Pocket Practice Guides

Interviewing and Recruiting Veterinary Staff

Maggie Shilcock
BSc CMS

Illustrated by Hayley Albrecht

Threshold Press

First published 2003 by
Threshold Press Ltd, 152 Craven Road
Newbury, Berks RG14 5NR
Phone: 01635-528375
email: publish@threshold-press.co.uk
www.threshold-press.co.uk

ISBN 1–903152–10–0

Typeset by Threshold Press Ltd
Printed in England by Biddles Ltd, Guildford and Kings Lynn

The Illustrator
Hayley Albrecht has been working full time as an artist and
illustrator for the last seven years. She specialises in animal
portraiture. Hayley has won numerous awards for her artwork and
exhibits in prestigious galleries countrywide and was recently
awarded associate membership to the Society of Equestrian
Artists. Special mention must go to Boot the dog who graced the
cover of the last Practice Guide. He managed to avoid the sausage
factory, I hope that he is enjoying being a git in heaven. He
deserves it!

Contents

List of Figures and Checklists

Figures

Checklists

1

The Recruitment Process

The aim of recruitment is to ensure that the organisation's demand for man and woman power is met by attracting potential employees in a cost-effective and timely manner. Put much more simply, when we recruit we are trying to get the right person for the job. Recruitment is however a complex process requiring a great deal of skill from those involved and mistakes can be costly

Employees are probably the greatest investment an organisation makes, so it is only sensible to choose wisely and carefully. The aim of any organisation should be to recruit only high quality people who will match the requirements of the job.

Why is recruitment so important?
There are two main reasons why recruitment is so important to the practice.

Firstly, finding the right people for the right job is essential to the smooth running of any practice. It makes sense to spend time and effort on recruitment to achieve this.

A poor recruit can be an expensive mistake for a practice in both financial terms and human terms. If at the end of the day the employee and practice have to part company, yet more time and money will have to be spent to find their replacement.

Although it is possible to part company with an unsatisfactory new employee in the first twelve months of their employment with reasonable ease, do remember that the twelve-month rule will not apply to discrimination claims. The sad fact is that many veterinary practices wait too long before making this decision and find that they are to all intents and purposes 'stuck' with a far from ideal member of staff. None of us like 'sacking' staff and while no recruitment process is fool-proof, the better the system, the more likely it will be that a good match of employee to job will result. Finding you have appointed the 'wrong' person is an expensive mistake, and the true cost of recruitment is discussed later in the chapter.

Poor recruitment policies leading to employment of unsuitable personnel also result in high labour turnover and/or poor standards of work as well as possible absenteeism – all of which increase your costs and damage the business of the practice. If the right people are recruited they are more likely to stay. If the wrong people are recruited they will either leave when they find more suitable employment, or when they are asked to leave before they have been with the practice for twelve months. Either way this can be viewed as time wasted in training and development, often for little return to the practice.

The second main reason to have a good recruitment system relates to the image of the practice and its standing in both the local and veterinary community.

Whenever a practice interviews for staff from the local community they are likely to be receiving applications from, and interviewing, existing or potential clients. People who are treated well when they seek employment with the practice are potential ambassadors, whether they are successful in their application or not. Conversely, those who are treated badly or are given a bad impression of the practice will be quick to spread the news and, as we all know, one person will tell at least ten others about a bad experience. It is therefore very important that advertising and interviewing procedures are well organised. Examples of poor organisation which would cause criticism from applicants would be:

- ◆ no reply to a job application or interview
- ◆ keeping interviewees waiting too long for their interview

◆ receptionists not knowing that the applicant has come for an interview
◆ an untidy, disorganised surgery.

Poor recruitment procedures for nurses and veterinary surgeons will have a similar effect as described above. The veterinary world is small, word passes quickly and ignoring applications, poor communication or a badly conducted interview will soon be related to vets and nurses who may have been potential future recruits.

The real cost of recruitment

Recruiting staff costs money. Poor recruitment and selection of staff costs even more money. So let's look at the real cost of employing a new member of staff.

Advertising

Most veterinary surgeon, veterinary nurse and practice manager jobs are advertised in the *Veterinary Record* and more recently the *Veterinary Times*. Generally adverts are placed in these journals for a number of weeks and although there are often special deals of four adverts for the price of three, the cost of advertising will be in the hundreds of pounds. The larger the advert the more expensive it will be.

Job adverts for support staff are usually placed in the situations vacant columns of local and regional newspapers. A boxed advert of only 30 words will cost in the region of £60, while unboxed adverts cost about ten pence per word.

Interviews

Interviewing candidates takes time. There is the working time of the interviewers to consider plus that of the staff who show the interviewees around the practice. If six candidates are each interviewed by two people for forty-five minutes and shown around the practice for fifteen minutes by a member of staff, the interview process has used twelve hours of staff time – well over £100 in salaries. If there are second interviews, yet more time will have to be costed out.

Administration
Consider the time and materials used in facilitating the interviews: letters sending job descriptions, letters offering interviews, letters of rejection, postage and the time of a member of staff to organise it all. We are again talking about a significant amount of money.

Planning
The planning stages of selection and interviewing take time. Those involved have to decide on and write the job description, the advert, the personal profile and the interview forms. This alone will add up to many hours of work and then there is the time spent discussing candidates and making the final choice.

Clothing and equipment
A new member of staff will require a uniform and, if they are a veterinary surgeon, at least some new equipment. Again we are talking about quite a few hundred pounds to fully equip this new recruit.

Induction
No new staff member should be thrown headlong into working on the first day. Many veterinary practices provide at least one full induction day, plus time for induction training over the first few weeks of the new employee's job. Costing out the time spent on induction by the new recruit and their trainer will show just how much this necessary but time-consuming exercise costs.

Probationary appraisals
Many practices carry out probationary appraisals with new staff at one, three and six months. This is very helpful in assessing the progress of the new member of staff and the training and support they need, but of course it also costs money both in interviewing and administrative time.

Dismissal
If at the end of it all, the new employee is just not for you and you dismiss them or they leave, then not only have you invested a large amount of money for very little reward but you have to start all over again with the costly recruitment process. It is also worth remembering that if the

employee has been poorly chosen and does not fit into the practice work patterns or team, it is quite possible that while they are still working for you the morale of the other staff will be adversely effected. In addition clients may not receive the service that they are used to expecting.

Both these scenarios are potentially very costly in terms of lower productivity and client loss.

Training

New employees require job training whether they are veterinary surgeons, nurses or receptionists. This may involve internal training sessions as well as external training courses, all of which is at a cost to the employer, not only in terms of course fees but also time away from the practice.

It is clear that recruitment costs should not be taken lightly. The practice is placing an investment in the recruitment and selection process and this is why it is so important to get it right. It is worth spending the time and the money if, at the end of the day, a good member of staff is appointed who works well with other staff, carries out their role efficiently and effectively and displays good client care skills.

There is one positive cost to recruitment. Today's restrictive legislation often means that, unless carefully handled, making changes to job descriptions for existing staff can be problematic. An employee's leaving provides a unique opportunity to re-design or re-structure a job to become more suitable to the needs of the practice, and thereby becoming a potentially more productive post.

The stages of recruitment

It is important to follow a logical recruitment process and not jump into the middle of the swimming pool before filling it with water. The stages of recruitment are shown below and will be dealt with in detail in the following chapters.

Do we need to recruit?

Do we need to replace the person leaving? Do we need to recruit for a new post?

What is the job we are recruiting for?

Do we need to re-assess the job description or design a new one?

Who do we want to recruit?

What sort of person do we need? What is the job profile we want for the ideal recruit?

What sort of advertisement do we need?
What do we want to say? How do we say it? Where do we want to place the advert?

How will we select the interviewees?
What criteria will we use? How many will we select to interview?

How will we carry out the interview?
Who will interview? How long will the interviews be? Will the interviewees be shown around the practice? What questions will we ask? Will there be a second interview?

What selection procedure will we use?
How will we select the right person? What criteria will we use? What references will we take up?

What acceptance and rejection procedures will we use?
What will we say in the acceptance letter? What will we say in the rejection letters?

The stages of recruitment   **Checklist**

Do we need to recruit?
What is the job?
Who do we want?
Advertising
Selecting interviewees
Interviewing
Final selection
Acceptance and rejection

Who is responsible for recruitment?

If a practice employs a practice manager, recruitment is very likely to be one of their responsibilities. In practices without a manager, the owner or a designated member of staff may take on this responsibility, perhaps with the help of a member of the administrative staff. In larger group practices a human resources manager may be employed to manage all personnel matters.

Although responsibility for recruitment may lie with these members of the practice, many other staff will have their part to play, whether it is showing a candidate around the practice, taking responsibility for paperwork and letters to candidates or acting as a second interviewer.

Figure 1
Recruitment Policy

(Practice name and logo)

Recruitment needs
- ❏ Is this a new post?
- ❏ Is this a replacement post?
- ❏ Is a new recruit required or can the post be filled internally, without advertising externally?

Job requirements
- ❏ Provide a full job description.

Personnel required
- ❏ Complete a personal profile and a skills profile for the job.

Advertising
- ❏ Decide on the design of the advert.
- ❏ Will a CV be requested or a job application form have to be filled in?
- ❏ Which veterinary journals or local/regional papers will be used?
- ❏ How long will advertisement be run?
- ❏ To whom will the applications be addressed?
- ❏ Will you give an e-mail address; if so, which one?

Selecting candidates for interview
- ❏ What criteria will be used for selection?
- ❏ How many candidates will be selected?

Interview letters
- ❏ Design the offer of interview letter.
- ❏ What will accompany the letter (practice brochure, job description, job application form, etc)?

Interviewing
- ❏ Who will interview?
- ❏ Where will interviews be held?
- ❏ How long will interviews be?
- ❏ Will candidates be shown around the practice? Will this be before or after the interview and who will do this?
- ❏ Will there be second interviews?

Selection procedure
- ❏ What criteria will be used for selection?
- ❏ Will an assessment form be used?
- ❏ How will the final decision be made?
- ❏ What references will be taken up?

Job offer letter
- ❏ Design of the letter (what information will it contain?)
- ❏ Will the job contract be sent with the letter?

Administration tasks
- ❏ Who will be responsible for the administrative tasks?
- ❏ What time scale will there be for completion of all tasks?
- ❏ What record keeping is required?

The practice recruitment policy

Life is made very much easier if there is a written practice recruitment policy, which is followed as a routine each time a vacancy or new post is to be filled and which can be maintained and improved in the light of experience.

The policy should be:

Efficient
Use cost efficient methods and make good use of the time allocated for recruitment.

Effective
Produce suitable candidates and identify appropriate people for the job.

Fair
Decisions should be based on the merits of individuals and with reference to discrimination and equal opportunities for all legislation.

Consistent
Use the same criteria for all job vacancies.

Simple
Kept as simple as possible to operate.

A simple recruitment policy can be designed by enlarging on the questions posed in the stages of recruitment section earlier in this chapter. You can produce your own basic policy by completing the questions posed in the outline recruitment policy in figure 1.

Summary

- Employees are the practice's greatest investment and should be recruited with care.
- Poor recruitment policies often result in poor staff.
- Poor recruitment procedures can result in bad PR for the practice.
- Recruitment is costly, but it is money well spent if the right staff are employed.
- Having a written staff recruitment policy aids the recruitment process.

2

The Job Description

Why have a job description?

If an employee has no job description, how will they know what they are supposed to do? If a post has no job description attached to it how does an employer know what an employee is supposed to do and that they are doing it? If there is no job description for a prospective new post how will the employer or potential new employee know what the job entails and how can it be advertised effectively? It is vital to have a very clear written description of the job you wish an employee to carry out.

The job description literally describes the job that needs to be done, but it also provides the information needed to write the job advert, design the selection criteria at the interview and create the personal and skills profile of the potential employee. If the post is not a new one any existing job description should be looked at very closely to assess if any parts of the job need changing or updating and if this is the case changes should be made to the job description.

Job adverts can normally only set out a very brief description of a post. It is good selection practice to include in the advert an invitation to apply for further job particulars. The information pack that is then sent out should include the job description as well as other general practice information. This ensures the interviewee has a very good idea of the job they are being interviewed for. Also an element of self-selection operates, and precious time is not wasted interviewing someone who discovers half way through the interview that this is not the job for them, or that the salary is not sufficient. If information packs are not

sent out then at the very least all candidates offered interviews should be sent a job description.

A clear job description helps to avoid misunderstandings at interview about the role of the employee both on the part of the candidate and the interviewer. It also ensures that the newly appointed staff understand the primary purpose and principal functions of the job and its place in the structure of the organisation.

Job descriptions clarify the role of the employee and set the boundaries of their job making it clear what their responsibilities are – and are not. They are also invaluable for the good management of appraisals, training and discipline. It is only by knowing what activities an employee should be carrying out that a manager can assess their competency and look at training needs and ways of developing their potential.

Why have a job description?   Checklist

Clarifies the role of the employee
Sets the boundaries of the job
Useful at appraisals
Useful for discipline

Who writes it?

The ideal person to write a job description is the person who actually does the job; after all they know best what they do. However, so that the job is tailored to the practice needs, it is best policy for the job description to be written by the person doing the job in collaboration with the practice manager or person responsible for personnel. If the job is new then the design of the job will fall to the manager who should consult the employees who will be working alongside the new recruit and who will have a very good idea of the requirements of the new post.

Veterinary practice is constantly changing which means that so too are the requirements of peoples' jobs. As jobs change new job descriptions will be required and these should be written with the agreement of, and in consultation with the employee whose job is altering.

What does it contain?

The job description should provide the answers to the questions:
◆ What is the job there for, why is it needed?
◆ What does it contribute to the practice's aims and objectives?
◆ How does it fit in to the practice's organisation of work and services?
◆ What are the job's main duties, responsibilities and/or accountabilities?

A job description should contain the following information.

Job title

The title of the job should be considered very carefully. Use words that describe the job. If the job has changed since the last appointment it may be appropriate to change its title. Many employees place a high importance on job title and potential applicants may be influenced by the status the job reflects. For example 'kennel assistant' may not sound as attractive as 'animal care assistant' even though the activities of the job could be very similar. The phrase 'What's in a name' could have great significance when choosing job titles.

The major purpose of the job

This statement sets the scene for the more detailed description later. It should make clear the major purpose and principal activities of the job. It is the statement that answers the question posed at the beginning of the section; what is the job there for and why is it needed?

So, for example, for a nurse's job the main purpose of the job may be defined as:

To act as a veterinary nurse in the practice nursing team, supplying surgical skills and animal nursing care to the practice small animal veterinary team and pet healthcare advice to clients.

Location of the job
The practice may have a number of sites so it is important that it is clear where the employee is expected to work. It may be that they are expected to provide cover at other sites even though they are based at a single site. If this is the case it should be made clear in this section of the job description.

Hours of work
The hours of work must be made very clear. State if overtime is required and what, if any sickness/holiday cover is expected.

Lines of authority
It is very important that the employee understands who it is that they are directly responsible to and to whom they should report. If they have a position of staff responsibility the job description should state which members of staff are responsible to them. Lines of authority need to be very clear so that no misunderstandings arise and staff positions within the practice are not undermined.

Main duties
In this section of the job description the main duties the post involves should be listed. Do not forget to include at the end of the list, 'Any other duties which may reasonably be required'. This allows for some flexibility in the job should the employer require other reasonable additional work – that is not on the job description – to be carried out. This could be, for example, if the practice is short-staffed or a specific task needs to be done for a short period of time. If however the employee's duties begin to alter significantly, a new job description should be agreed between employer and employee.

Knowledge and skills required
This is a simple statement of the skills required to fulfil the role. It can be very helpful during appraisal of the employee when their need for

Figure 2	**Job description for a veterinary receptionist**

Job Description

Title
Receptionist

Major purpose of job
To act as a member of the receptionist team providing a friendly, efficient and caring service to the practice clients

Location of job
The job is based at the main surgery

Hours of work
8.30 am–1.00 pm Monday–Friday
Overtime may be required

Lines of authority
Responsible to the Head Receptionist

Main duties
To answer telephone enquires
To book appointments
To maintain computerised client records
To give advice to clients on basic veterinary health care including feeding
To issue bills to clients and take payments
To cash up
To send out booster and other client reminders and information
To help produce waiting room displays

Knowledge and skills required
A sound knowledge of practice policies and protocols
Good client care skills
Good telephone skills
Competence in use of computer
Up-to-date knowledge of practice services and products
Sound knowledge of basic veterinary terms
Basic knowledge of common veterinary treatments and procedures

Training
Attendance at relevant in-house training sessions
Attendance at appropriate external training courses which will improve or enhance skills and personal development

further training and development is discussed.

Training
It should be made clear what training will be provided and what training the employee is expected to undertake as part of the job.

An example of a job description for a veterinary receptionist is shown in figure 2. The headings in the job description can of course be used to set out the job description of any veterinary employee.

Summary

- A job description is essential for designing the job, the advert and the personal specification.
- Job descriptions establish job duties boundaries and responsibilities, make clear lines of authority and avoid misunderstandings between employee and employer.
- The job description should be written by the employee carrying out the job and the practice/personnel manager.
- As jobs change so the job description should be altered with the agreement of the employee.

What the interviewees say

Maeve – Veterinary Surgeon   *Rowena – Receptionist*
Vanessa – Nurse/Receptionist   *Lisa – Nurse*

Q: Was it useful to see the job description before the interview and why?
Maeve – Yes, many jobs need a lot more following up as you get very little information and it is difficult to tell what they really involve until the interview.
Vanessa – Yes, the job can often be different from how the advert describes it. Seeing the job description before the interview means your time isn't wasted at an interview if the job is not what you want.
Rowena – Yes. I was impressed we were given one.
Lisa – Yes I felt very unprepared and the job description provided lots of details of the job. It helped me to prepare my questions and put me more at ease because I at least knew a lot about the job I was applying for.

Q: Did it clarify the job?

Vanessa – Yes because I had very little idea from the advert how much nursing I might be expected to do.

Rowena – Yes I had a good idea of the sort of job I was applying for.

Lisa – Yes, like Rowena it helped me to get a much better idea of what the job was all about.

3

The Person for the Job

The whole object of interviewing and recruitment is to find the right person for the job. This means finding someone who not only fits the technical needs of the job, i.e. has the necessary skills to carry out the job but who will also fit in with the practice's existing team of employees. Finding someone with both these qualities can often be difficult. You may find at interview someone with exactly the right skills and experience to do the job you are advertising, but who will not fit in with the rest of your staff. Conversely you may find the perfect team member but they lack all the necessary skills you require. Neither of these candidates will be the right person for the job.

It is very important to have a clear idea of the skills and personal qualities you require from this new employee before you make any attempt to select candidates for interview. A candidate profile enables you to set out these qualities and skills in a logical manner.

Candidate profile
This profile defines the skills, abilities, attributes and behaviour that you are looking for in the successful candidate. It is of immense use when selecting candidates for interview and for assessing them at the interview itself.

Start designing the profile by looking at the job description. Consider how the job may have changed since it was last advertised and how any changes will affect your needs in a new employee. Think also about their contact with clients, the personnel the new employee will be working with and what sort of person you need to fit into this existing team.

The profile can be broken down into a number of qualities.

Personality

Do you want someone who looks smart and tidy? Does it matter how clearly they speak? Almost all veterinary staff will be dealing with clients so these two qualities are very important. What sort of personality do you require, bearing in mind the other staff they will be working with and the impression you want to give clients of the practice?

Disposition

Can they use their own initiative? How enthusiastic are they about the job and, just as important in a veterinary practice environment, how resilient are they?

Interpersonal skills

How good are their communication and rapport-building skills?

Flexibility

Will you require overtime or weekend work? Do you want someone who can cover for sickness at short notice?

Health and fitness

Will they be required to lift and carry? Do you anticipate that they will be working with large animals?

Driving licence

Does the job require someone who can drive and if so does the candidate hold a current and clean driving licence?

Travelling time

How far away from work is it acceptable for them to live if they are going to be on call?

Education

What qualifications do they need to carry out the job? Do you want a qualified nurse or a trainee? Do you want a vet with a particular certificate?

Work experience

What previous experience is required?

Specialist skills

Are there any specific skills required, e.g. computer skills, surgical skills?

Special work interests

Does the job require them to have a particular interest in, or develop a particular aspect of it?

Special circumstances

Will the job require the candidate to travel e.g. between surgeries, to conferences, meetings? Will it require overnight stays?

There are as many different specifications as there are jobs but if you aim to cover the general profile structure given in figure 3, you will have the minimum criteria to consider and can adapt your profile to suit the needs of the practice.

When you have decided upon the skills you require it is very helpful to set them out in the form of a table as shown in figure 3, giving a brief description of what you require under each heading. Beside each requirement place three other columns headed essential, desirable and contra-indicators.

⇨ Essential criteria are those that the candidate must have, for example, a V N qualification, or good telephone skills.

⇨ Desirable criteria are those that would be an added advantage, for example, a nurse with experience in holding puppy parties would be very useful but not essential.

⇨ Contra-indicators are things that genuinely disqualify someone from being able to do the job. For example, you may require a nurse who can help with X-raying and therefore there will be an age limit below which candidates will not be acceptable.

However you should be very careful to avoid falling into the trap of discrimination here, especially with regard to disability and equal opportunities. So any factors which will disqualify a candidate must be fully justifiable and legal.

A word here about discrimination. It can be very easy to

Figure 3	Skills and personal profile		
	Essential	Desirable	Contra-indicators
Personality What does the job demand in terms of smartness and manner?			
Disposition Does the job require initiative and enthusiasm? Does the person need to be able to work on their own?			
Interpersonal skills Will the person need to deal with clients and work as a team member? Are good communication skills required?			
Flexibility Does the job require overtime or night or weekend duty to be carried out? Will the person be working at more than one site?			
Health and fitness Does the job have any physical requirements such as lifting or working with large animals?			
Travelling time If the person is going to be on duty, is there a maximum distance they should live from work in order to fulfil their duty requirements?			
Education What educational qualifications and job knowledge is required?			
Work experience What previous experience is needed?			
Specialist skills and interests What specific skills are required?			
Special circumstances Does the job require special travelling or overnight stays?			

become entangled in the area of discrimination during profiling and selecting as well as interviewing. The active avoidance of discrimination should run throughout the whole recruitment process and will be discussed in various chapters of this book. The consequences of discrimination can be serious and lead to heavy legal costs if the employer is seen to have been discriminatory towards a candidate.

At the profiling stage care must be taken when specifying particular qualities and skills required by the candidates that discrimination is not implied. In its simplest form you cannot specify whether you want a male or a female vet to fill the post or what nationality you wish them to be.

It is always wise to seek legal advice on any employment matters and there are a number of free legal advice lines available to the veterinary profession. Examples of these advice lines are available to members of the British Veterinary Association (BVA), British Small Animal Veterinary Association (BSAVA), the Veterinary Practice Management Association (VPMA) and the Federation of Small Businesses (FSB).

Summary

- The right candidate must not only have the correct technical skills but must also be able to fit in with the practice team.
- Designing a candidate profile enables the interviewers to establish the skills, abilities, attributes and behaviour required of the successful candidate.
- A candidate profile form can be very helpful for use when selecting candidates for interview and when interviewing.
- Always avoid discrimination when designing the profile.

What the interviewers say

Q: How does the personal profile help with interviewing?

Mary – It means we have a standard to compare the interviewees with, and more important that we have thought very carefully about the job and the sort of person we want to recruit before the actual interview. Of course you have to be flexible and we never find someone who exactly fits the profile, interviewing is never that perfect.

Denise – It provides me with an 'ideal' person for the job, it makes me think beforehand about what sort of person I am looking for.

4

Advertising

If you look in the major veterinary journals you will find an almost infinite variety of advertisements for veterinary surgeons, nurses and practice managers. The same applies to the adverts in local newspapers for veterinary receptionists. Before you design your own advertisement look at all these other ones very carefully. What catches your eye? Which adverts are you drawn to? Is it the size, the logo, the fact that the advert is boxed, or the first line of the advert that makes it stand out?

The important point to remember is that none of these things are actually telling you about the job itself – they are simply means of attracting your eye to the advert so that you then read further. An effective advert needs to have visual impact as well as containing the appropriate job information. It should not oversell the job however, as there is no point in painting a rosy picture of a job which in reality is not all that it is made out to be. The new employee will soon discover this and may well leave at the first opportunity placing the practice back at square one, having to start the recruitment process all over again. The advertisement is the key link between the recruitment and selection of candidates, and its aim is to produce a compact field of candidates capable of doing the job.

Designing the advertisement

It is almost impossible to design the perfect advert. The difficulty is that different people will be attracted by different things. A veterinary surgeon who wants to work in Somerset may well be attracted by an advert that places location at the head of the advert, while a vet who is happy to work in any part of the country may in fact look for adverts that simply have 'veterinary surgeon wanted' as their headline. Some candidates will be attracted by a logo, some by the strapline or wording of the first few sentences of the advert, while others will religiously read every advert word by word. In just one issue of *Veterinary Times* the adverts for veterinary nurses had the following headers:

Northern Ireland – Head Nurse Required

VN Required

Going to the Commonwealth Games this Summer?

East Midlands Veterinary Clinic offers exciting opportunity

Senior qualified nursing positions

Exciting opportunity in Scotland

VN Needed

Ever wanted to join the circus?

Essex Qualified VN Required

Do You Want a Real Change of Scene?

Kate is expecting so…

On there own some of these headings don't even make sense, but they do catch the eye and imagination, and for many job seekers encourage further investigation. The old idea of placing the title of the job as the header is fast disappearing and 'quirky' headers are increasingly being used to attract the attention of job seekers. It is probably reasonable to expect that the fewer candidates there are in the job market the more outrageous will become the headlines of the adverts!

The aim of the advert is to attract the 'target group' of candidates at the least cost and with the greatest effectiveness. At the end of the day, the exact wording and the headers that you use have to be what you think will attract the sort of candidate you are looking for.

Whatever first line you chose for your advert, the content will also require a number of essential ingredients in order to attract the potential applicant. There are no firm rules about the order in which this information is placed, but the checklist provides an example of a logical sequence of information which could be placed in any job advert.

Size and shape of advert

The bigger the advert the more likely it is that it will attract attention and of course the more it will cost. However, in these days of veterinary surgeon and veterinary nurse shortages a large advert may well be a good investment. A boxed advert is easier to see and read, it stands out better than simple text and looks smarter. Adverts which are two columns wide are also better to read than long single column adverts as the eye scans across the double column more easily.

Practice logo or name

If the practice has a logo then use it in the advert. A logo will attract the reader's eye but be careful, if you have an intricate logo, that it is large enough to read in what is a relatively small advertising space. Simple logos can be much more effective in adverts. Remember also

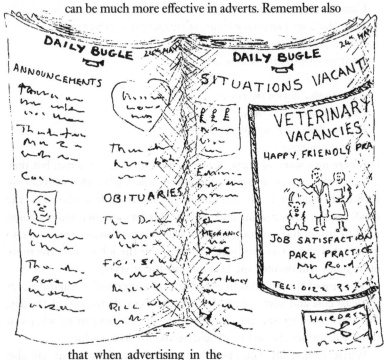

that when advertising in the local press the name of the practice will be known by many of the readers and therefore have more impact than in a national advert.

Job title

This is more important than you may think. Consider the job title carefully and use words that are descriptive of the job, e.g. Senior Surgical Nurse gives more information than VN. If the job has changed since the last appointment the title may need to be changed to better describe what it now entails. Many employees place a high importance on job title and potential applicants may well be influenced by the status the title reflects.

About the practice
Provide any relevant information about the practice which you think will attract the reader, but don't go overboard and write an essay on your client care or surgical equipment, etc. First this will make the advert expensive and secondly, the reader will probably give up half way through.

Put in what you think are selling points; for example, this may be the location if the practice is in a very attractive part of the country. It may be the modern equipment or the fact that the practice has just been refurbished, or perhaps the fact that the practice has gained Investors in People. This is a good point to confirm that the practice is committed to equal opportunities in employment.

About the job
Describe the job in such a way that the potential applicant gains a very clear idea of what it really involves. State the main duties and responsibilities, hours worked, location, duty rotas and if overtime will be required. A clear description of the job in the advert will weed out some unsuitable applicants as well as encourage more promising candidates.

The person required
Use the person profile (discussed in chapter 3) to write this section. Make it brief, but be clear what qualities you are looking for in the candidate.

The benefits
State any benefits that go with the job. These may be benefits such as uniform, health care insurance, sickness/disability insurance, housing and car.

CV and application forms
State whether you wish the applicant to send in a curriculum vitae or request an application form from the practice.

Contact details
Provide contact details, this may be a name and address, a telephone number, an email address or all three.

Closing date
Give a closing date for applications. This helps you to organise the interviewing as well as avoiding disappointment for applicants who

contact the practice only to find that the post has been filled.

Discrimination

Consider the two excerpts from advertisements below.

a *We require a tall, friendly, attractive blonde in her twenties to work as a receptionist in our busy veterinary practice.*

b *Veterinary receptionist required for our busy veterinary practice. The successful applicant should have some experience of reception work and good people skills.*

It's fairly obvious here which of these two extracts is discriminatory! The qualities in (a) may well be on some owner's 'wish list' but to ask for them in an advert is a highly discriminatory description of the type of person required for the post. 'Tall', 'attractive' and 'blonde' could all be used as examples of discrimination and it is likely that in the not too distant future the specification of an age requirement will join them.

The job advert   Checklist

Advert header – optional
Logo or practice name
Job title
Practice information
Job information
The person required
The benefits provided
CV or application form
Contact details
Closing date

Always consider the legal aspects when designing the job advert. Avoid discrimination, in particular be careful regarding discrimination against gender, race and age. Particularly don't use the words 'he' or 'she', or job titles that specify gender like 'kennel maid'. Avoid stipulating characteristics that exclude potential applicants of any sex or race or particular age range and if in any doubt seek legal advice.

Where to advertise

It is important to consider both internal as well as external advertising. It may be that just the right person for the job is already working for you.

Internal advertising

In larger companies it is often a matter of policy to notify employees of vacancies. It can be a great waste of resources not to make use of appropriate internal people. Additionally, seeing that opportunities are filled internally can be very motivating for an employee who wishes to progress and increase job skills and responsibilities. Hopefully, if the practice carries out an appraisal system, managers will be aware of the potential of their employees, and have a very good idea if there is anyone already in the practice who could do the job there is now a vacancy for.

The advantages of recruiting internally are that the candidates have an existing track record, they are familiar with the practice and how it runs and presumably get on well with existing staff. However be careful not to recruit in this way simply because it is the easy option and saves the practice money. If these are the primary reasons for appointing an internal candidate you could be making a costly mistake.

External recruitment

Traditionally this is by advertising in the relevant professional journals such as *The Veterinary Record* and more recently *The Veterinary Times* for veterinary surgeons, veterinary nurses and practice managers. Local and regional press are normally used for recruiting administrative and reception staff. As discussed in chapter 1, the cost of advertising is often high – so all the more reason for making sure you have a well designed advert that is effective in attracting the right candidates. There is no set period for the length of time an advert is run; really it must be run for as long as it takes to find the right person for the job. Many publications offer deals for multiple-week advertising, but one advert for one week may be sufficient if the employment market is overflowing with the sort of employee you are looking for.

In reality you will probably have to advertise professional posts for a number of weeks to ensure the maximum exposure of the advert. If this is the case, take care not to grab the first likely applicant and offer them the job. There may be others better qualified who will apply two weeks down the line and it would be a pity to have missed them through being too hasty.

Recommendation

Using recommendations is another way to recruit. Friends and colleagues may well provide contacts with potential candidates. It is always important under these circumstances to still ask the recommended applicant to officially apply for the job and for the employer to remain totally objective about their selection. Just because they are known to a colleague does not mean they are automatically the person for the job. Even more difficult can be the relative who is recommended for the post.

The practice may have a policy on employing relatives of existing employees, while in other practices, relatives will not be employed simply because of the potential problems and embarrassments that could occur. As with any other recommended candidate if you are to consider a relative treat them as you would any other applicant, and do not employ them just because it would upset their already employed brother or cousin if you did not.

Recruitment agencies

The use of recruitment agencies can significantly reduce the time spent sifting through application forms and CVs and replying to applicants. The agency will produce for you, for a fee, a shortlist of the most suitable candidates from which you can select those you wish to interview. If you do consider using a recruitment agency make sure you use one which will cater for your specific requirements and has a good track record in veterinary recruitment.

CVs and application forms

Whether you request an applicant to provide a CV or complete an application form is a matter of choice for each practice. Both have their advantages and disadvantages.

CVs

The curriculum vitae provided by the candidate may provide you with a wealth of information or alternatively very little, and often not the kind of information you need to make a good assessment of the candidate. You have no control over what information is provided.

Many CVs appear to be clones of each other having been compiled using standard wording or perhaps from a computer programme. They are often packed full of the latest management 'buzz phrases' such as, team player, highly motivated, assertive and so on. Some CVs come in folders with pictures but not much else, while others provide relevant useful information. However CVs do have some advantages over an application form, because they do allow more free expression from the candidate. This can sometimes provide the selector with more useful information than from a poorly designed application form.

Application forms

Application forms have a number of advantages over CVs as long as they are well designed. The standardised format of the form allows for an easier comparison between candidates and it is also easier to develop specific questions for interview. Another important advantage is that an application form allows the candidate an opportunity to decide if they match up to the job requirements stated on the form, and in this way it acts as a good pre-screening device, as some candidates may well de-select themselves.

Many application forms are poorly designed, asking the applicant too few or irrelevant questions, or in some cases are so involved and complicated that the selectors are faced with a mass of information to sift through, much of which is unnecessary.

It may be stating the obvious but it is very important to be sure that you design the application form to give the information you need. Design the form to relate to the job. If the practice already has a standard application form, review it first and make sure that it requests all the information that you need to know from the applicants for this particular vacancy.

Base the content of the form as closely as you can on the job description and person specification you have already designed so that it is also being used as a pre-screening mechanism. Candidates who find that they cannot answer some of the questions on the form, or that many of the job requirements or questions are not relevant to their skills, may simply not return the form, thus saving both your and their time. Hopefully those who do return the form will be fulfilling all the basic requirements of the job and therefore making your selection task a little easier.

Figure 4 is an example of an application form designed to be used for a specific job. What is placed in the job requirements section will depend on the nature of the post and should be altered for each post advertised.

Application forms never seem to provide enough space to write in. Try to be generous with space, after all you want as much information as possible from the candidate at a legible size, and not tiny writing

Figure 4   Application form

Application for post of   (Title of post)

Name
Address
Contact details

Education
Please give details of educational
attainments listing dates and
qualifications starting with the
most recent

Employment record
Starting with your current post please
list the jobs you have held over the
last x years and give details of:
  Employer
  Dates when you were employed the
  nature of the job and main duties
  Your achievements in the post
  Reason for leaving the post

Job requirements
Please describe how you meet
(List here the job requirements
from the job description and
personal skills from e.g.
  Professional/job knowledge
  Management skills
  Communication skills
  Personal skills)

Health
Number of days sickness in last
two years
Please give reasons for sickness.
Are you aware of any medical
condition which may affect your ability
to undertake the full duties of
the post safely and without risk to
your health? (If yes, please give details)
Are you likely to require any
adjustments to the premises or working arrangements to be made on
account of disability of any kind?
(If yes, please give details)

Work Permit
Are you legally able to work in the UK?
Please give permit details

Convictions
Please give details of any criminal convictions

Interests and hobbies
Please list your outside
interests and hobbies

Additional information
Please list here any additional
information which you think relevant
to your application for this post

Declaration
I declare that the information given in
this application form is accurate
Date.................... Signature...

---

squashed into a small box that you have to read with a magnifying glass. Alternatively make a note in each section of the form suggesting the candidate puts extra information on a separate piece of paper. When sending the form to the applicant enclose a copy of the job description so that they have a very clear idea of the job and are therefore able to complete the application form more easily.

The letter of application

It can be very helpful to read a candidate's letter of application for a post advertised, especially if the only other application document is a CV. Many job adverts will request 'a letter of application and CV'. The letter enables the selectors to find out a little more about the candidate. Their handwriting, grammar, the phrases and words they use and the general layout of the letter all help to give a picture of the potential interviewee. Of course many letters will be produced on word processors and only signatures will be 'hand written'. The letter should ideally set out why the applicant wants the job and not just say, 'I wish to apply for the job advertised...'

Look at the writing paper that is used, most selectors have in their time received letters of application on note paper torn from an exercise pad or, worse still, from a spiral-bound notebook. What does this say about the candidate's attitude to the job? Certainly it suggests they have not given the matter much time or consideration nor do they consider the job important enough to warrant decent notepaper.

If you manage the advertising of the job correctly and send out well-structured application forms, or request detailed CVs accompanied by a letter of application, you will hopefully receive applications from suitably qualified people. You will then be in the best position possible to select the most suitable candidates for interview.

Summary

- It is impossible to design the 'perfect' advert as different people will be attracted by different information.
- Before designing the advert look at the format of adverts offering similar jobs.
- The aim of the advert is to attract a target group of applicants.
- An advert should contain a number of essential ingredients which will include job title, practice information, job details, job benefits, the type of person required, how to apply and contact details.
- Consider both internal and external advertising, personal recommendation and recruitment agencies when looking for new staff.
- Decide whether an application form will be sent to all applicants or whether a CV will be sufficient for the information you require about the candidates.
- Always read the letter of application carefully; it can tell you a lot about the candidate.

What the interviewees say

Maeve – Veterinary Surgeon   *Rowena – Receptionist*
Vanessa – Nurse/Receptionist   *Lisa – Nurse*

Q: What sort of adverts attract you?
Maeve – Actually I just look through all the adverts regardless of size or shape.
Vanessa – Big bold ones and ones, I like to be able to scan the adverts easily for the job headings.
Rowena – Bold titles.

Q: Did the advert attract you?

Maeve – Yes, because it give me information about the practice, the number of vets, it sounded the sort of place I wanted to work and gave me enough information to decide to apply for the position.

Rowena – Yes. I saw the name of the surgery and that was what attracted me.

Lisa – I liked the way it was written, it didn't look scary and I felt happy to apply for it.

Vanessa – It was an attractive advert and I felt I could apply for the job even though I am older, it sounded very welcoming.

Q: Is the job what you expected it would be from the advert?

Maeve – Yes, it is very much as I expected form the advert and of course I also received a practice profile when I initially made enquiries so this helped a great deal as well.

Lisa – Yes, but since I have been working at the practice I now have a lot more responsibility which is great.

Vanessa – Well, it was only when I read the job description that I realised what a veterinary receptionist's job really entailed.

5

Selecting for Interview

You've advertised the post and hopefully have had a positive response from the sort of candidates you are looking for. Now is the time to set in motion the selection process which will identify those candidates you think it is worthwhile to interview. It is important to establish the criteria to use for selection so that you are comparing like candidate with like candidate.

Selection criteria

The selection criteria will be a combination of job description requirements and personal profile requirements. Consider how well the applicant measures up to the personal profile you drew up for the ideal person for the job. Is the applicant likely to be able to carry out the job description you have designed? To be able to make these decisions you need to be able to assess the evidence they have supplied in the form of CVs, completed application forms, letters of application and the occasional recommendation you have received.

Assessing CVs and application forms
CVs

Although most people are truthful when compiling their CV, some can be economical with the truth, or perhaps omit negative facts, fail to make clear certain periods of unemployment or perhaps exaggerate achievements. The CV needs to be carefully analysed. A well-structured CV will tell you quite a lot about the candidate's ability to organise and communicate facts. The CV should be concise and contain educational and career histories in reverse chronological order. This enables the selector to see the most recent activities first. We have already discussed the variety of CVs which might be received, the important thing is that they present information in a logical and easily understood manner.

Having read the CV, consider whether the applicant has the qualifications and work experience required.

⇨ Do they have any other useful skills?
⇨ How has their career progressed?
⇨ How long have they stayed in each job, and does this give you any indication of how long they may stay with the practice?
⇨ Do they appear to be making a logical career move?
⇨ Can you build up a picture of the applicant from their CV; does it leave you with a positive impression?

Make notes of items of specific interest which you may wish to discuss at an interview and look very carefully for any inconsistencies in the CV or gaps in employment. If there are gaps in the employment record, try to establish if the reasons are explained elsewhere, e.g. a holiday break, illness etc. If there is no obvious reason for the gap then this is an area for questioning, should you wish to interview the applicant. Look at hobbies and interests, does the applicant appear to be the sort of person who is likely to 'fit in' with existing staff and the locality?

Application forms

It is easier to analyse application forms because the consistency of questioning means that all applicants will have had to answer the same questions and it is therefore much

Figure 5

Job applicants comparison table

(1 is low, 2 is average, 3 is good)

Applicant	Education			Job knowledge			Experience			Special aptitudes			General impression		
	1	2	3	1	2	3	1	2	3	1	2	3	1	2	3
Mary Brown		✳			✳			✳				✳	✳		
James Green			✳			✳			✳		✳				✳

easier to make comparisons. Use the same criteria as for assessing C V s; look for inconsistencies, contradictions and gaps. Also take note of the personal statement section where the applicant has been asked to give additional information to back up their application and reasons why they are the right person for the job. Have they managed to convince you they are the person you need?

Assessing letters of application
Reading letters of application can be useful for assessment. A well-structured letter indicates an organised mind and may supply you with information that neither the C V nor application form can. The letter may give you a glimpse of the character of the applicant through their free use of words rather than the stilted text provided in CVs and application forms.

Assessing personal recommendations
Take into account any personal recommendations. As we have seen in the previous chapter these can be fraught with difficulties but at the same time, if a colleague does know of someone who they think would be 'just right for the job', this may help you in your selection process.

It is always very important to look at the reasons the candidate gives for leaving not just their present job, but also previous jobs. A well-presented C V should provide this information and an application form should ask for it. The reasons given can provide you with a lot of information. If the reason given is not enough money, do check that you are offering a salary that is likely to be acceptable. If you are not, and do not wish to increase it for this particular applicant, then do not put them on your interview list even if they fulfil all the other criteria. Where boredom is given as a reason for leaving, will this job bore them as well? If they are ambitious to move up and on in their career, will the job provide them with this opportunity? Or does it appear that they are restless, moving from job to job after relatively short periods of time? If so, will they leave this job in the same manner just as you have managed to fully train them?

Selecting candidates
Having looked at and assessed all the applications you must now make the decision about whom to interview. Unless you have a very small

number of applicants you cannot interview them all, so a shortlist must be drawn up. It can be very useful to draw up a comparisons table as shown in figure 5. Grade the qualities you require (taken from the personal profile) and complete the comparisons table. Once you have done this it should be fairly obvious which applicants to interview. Whether you use this comparison system or simply use your judgement, the next step is to place each application in one of three piles.

⇨ Pile number one is for applicants you want to interview, those who meet and maybe exceed the criteria you have specified and you feel have that something extra that makes them worthy of interview.

⇨ Pile number two is for applicants who generally meet all the criteria but are not so outstanding. These are the applicants who you may promote to pile one if you are short of candidates to interview.

⇨ Pile number three is for applicants who do not satisfy the criteria required, they are not the people for you and should at this stage be sent letters thanking them for applying for the job but stating that they have not been successful in their application.

It is often worthwhile including in your shortlist for interview one or two applicants who have special or exceptional skills or who simply seem to stand out from the others, even though they may have some short comings as all-rounders. It may depend on the post you want to fill, but it is sometimes worth interviewing a couple of unconventional candidates – the 'wild cards' – they may turn out to be ideal for the job.

Having chosen the candidates, they should be contacted and offered an interview. To save time, some practices telephone candidates to offer the interview and fix the interview time. Others send letters offering an interview and an example of an interview letter is shown in figure 6. There are no hard and fast rules here as long as the date, time and place of the interview are made quite clear. It is important, however, that each candidate receives a job description before the interview. Those who completed job application forms will have already seen the job description enclosed with the application form, but candidates who simply sent in a CV will not have had that opportunity. The job description gives the candidate more information about the job and enables them to think of questions that they may wish to ask. The salary should be included in the job description, if it has not been stated in the job advert (and it is very likely that it has not been).

You now have to wait and to see if your selection procedures have been successful. If you have clearly defined your needs for the new recruit, and carefully assessed the applications, you should be presented with a group of interviewees who are more than capable of doing the job and also meet the personal specifications required for them to fit in with the other staff.

However, be warned, there always seems to be someone who gets through the screening net and causes your heart to sink when you start to interview them. They are the mistakes and we all make them, however experienced one becomes at selecting candidates.

Figure 6   **Sample interview letter**

Title of post

Address

Date

Dear ....

Thank you for applying for the above position. We would like you to attend for interview at 10am on Thursday 24th September at the above address. This will be an informal interview with the Practice Manger and Head Nurse and will last approximately one hour.
When you arrive please go to our reception area and give the receptionist your name, she will be expecting you. I enclose a practice brochure which contains a map showing how to find the practice.
Could you please confirm that you will be attending the interview. If there are any difficulties or you have any queries please do not hesitate to contact me.
I look forward to meeting you on 24th September

Yours sincerely

Name...........................
Practice Manager

Summary
- Decide carefully what selection criteria you are going to use to choose the candidates for interview.
- Decide how many candidates you wish to interview.
- Assess applications using CVs, application forms, personal recommendations and the letters of application.

- Divide the applications into three piles:
    - pile one   applicants to interview
    - pile two   possible interviews
    - pile three   no interview.
- It is often worthwhile throwing in a 'wild card' interviewee.
- Telephoning the candidates to fix interviews often saves time.
- You will not always get the selection process right, be prepared for the occasional disappointment.

What the interviewers say

Q: How do you choose candidates for interview?

Mary – By comparing the personal profile and job requirements with the application letters. I also throw in a 'wild card' each time – you just never know if you might have missed the right person. I also look at how neat the applications are and how much trouble they have taken with the application.

Q: Are the letters of application usually like the people?

Denise – No, there are often surprises.

Mary – You have a picture in your mind of what they will be like and how they will look. They are rarely how you imagine.

Q: Do you ever get it totally wrong?

Mary – Yes, of course.

Denise – Yes, although I am getting better at selecting.

Q: What about the candidates you didn't interview?

Denise – Who knows? We can't interview everyone, so we have to trust our judgement and not worry about whether or not we have missed a really good person.

Mary – You mustn't worry about it.

6

Preparing for the Interview

Interviewing will always be more successful if the whole procedure is well planned beforehand. A badly prepared interview will be obvious to most candidates and does not provide a very good advertisement for the organisation of the practice. Nor will it be very efficient in selecting the right person for the job. It is important to consider all the aspects of the interview and how you are going to achieve the best possible scenario for selecting your new vet, nurse or receptionist.

Interviewing is not easy and it takes up lot of time, so it is important to think carefully how you are going to organise the exercise. You need to be sure of the information, paperwork and resources you need and the help required from other members of staff, if you are going to make it successful.

What is the objective of the interview?
If you don't have a clear idea of what the objectives of the interview are it will be difficult to choose the right candidate. The following might be some of your objectives.
⇨ To find out if the candidate is suitable for the job.
⇨ To find out if the job is suitable for the candidate.
⇨ To ensure all candidates have a fair interview.
⇨ To interview all candidates the same manner to enable a fair comparison.
⇨ To treat all candidates in such a way as to put over a positive image of the practice.

Who is going to interview?

The best people to interview candidates are the practice manager or person responsible for personnel matters and the potential employee's immediate supervisor. Generally two interviewers will be sufficient, too many interviewers can be daunting and for many jobs are simply overkill. However, for some more responsible jobs such as veterinary surgeons, head nurses or head receptionists a third interviewer may be beneficial. So, for example, two partners and the practice manager may interview a vet, while the practice manager, senior partner and partner responsible for small animal work may interview for a head nurse, – for a general nursing post the head nurse and practice manager would be sufficient.

How will the interviewers prepare themselves?

Very big mistakes can be made if the interviewers are not prepared or do not have at least some basic knowledge of interview techniques. Any member of staff who is likely to be interviewing on a regular basis would benefit from some interviewing training, while those who interview only occasionally certainly need some coaching from more experienced members of staff.

At the very least all interviewers should have read the applications of the candidates to be interviewed and be very familiar with the post being applied for, having looked at the job description and the personal profile of the ideal candidate. They should be sure of the objectives of the interview and how it is going to be carried out and what questions they will be asking. They should also consider how they will dress for the interview and what impression they wish to make on the candidate. Hopefully the candidate will have taken trouble to dress smartly, the interviewers should be courteous enough to do the same.

Will a member of staff show the candidates around the practice?

It is a very good idea to have a member of staff (ideally from the area where the candidate may be working), to show the candidate around the practice for twenty minutes or so before the formal interview takes place. This helps to put the interviewee at their ease, gives them some idea of how the practice operates and how it looks, and provides them with more material for asking questions. From the practice's point of view, it in effect provides another less formal interview and the member of staff is able to assess how well the candidate may get on with other personnel. Also, it is remarkable what candidates will tell the person showing them around the practice that they do not mention to the formal interviewers. Jobs have been lost in this way due to a casual remark such as, 'Oh, if I have a late night I phone in sick the next day' or 'I didn't take any notice of that rule in my last practice'.

Will you have second interviews?

It is standard procedure in some practices to have second interviews. This can be a good idea if you wish more members of staff to meet candidates or have interviewed a larger number and now have a short list of say three. It certainly gives you a second chance to assess the candidate and perhaps confirm you initial feelings on their suitability. If you have the time and resources this may be an option but for most posts is not strictly necessary.

How long will the interviews be?

You need to know how long the interviews will be in order to plan the interview day. In most cases 45 minutes of formal interview is sufficient, although the candidate may then go on to meet other staff or have lunch with some of them, etc. This is often the case with veterinary surgeon interviews, and of course the candidate may well have already had an 'informal' interview with the person who has shown them around the practice.

Always give yourself at least fifteen minutes to gather your thoughts about the interview and complete the assessment form before passing on to the next candidate.

The golden rule is keep to time. Do not let the interviews over run. This means that some candidates will have had more than their fair share of interviewing, the objective of treating everyone the same has been lost and, probably worst of all, you then start running late, candidates are kept waiting, you start rushing and the interview procedure begins to collapse.

Where will the interviews be held?

The interviews must be held away from the main bustle of the practice. They should take place in a quiet calm environment where everyone can concentrate on the job in hand and not be disturbed by barking dogs or ringing telephones. Try to create an informal atmosphere. Avoid if possible having a desk, but if you do have one, do not place the candidate on one side and the interviewers on the other. Comfortable seating and a small coffee table are more appropriate and will help to put the candidate at their ease.

Try to avoid other distractions such as the sun in the candidate's eyes, a room that is too hot or too cold, noise, or an interesting view over the car park where clients can be watched taking their pets into the reception area. The room should be clean and tidy, remember you are trying to create an impression on the candidate too. Decide where you want the candidate to sit and when they enter the room indicate the chair that is for them. This prevents embarrassment and leaves you in control. Avoid the so-called booby traps like wobbly chairs, collapsing hat stands, the practice cat or dog being in the interview room ready to jump onto the candidate's knee and coffee served in a cup and saucer rather than a mug.

Do all the necessary staff know about the interviews?

Make sure that all those staff who need to know about the interviewing do so. This is especially important for the receptionists who are on duty that day. It is a poor reflection on the practice if the candidate arrives and the receptionist simply hasn't a clue who they are. Likewise if the candidate is being shown around the practice it is better for staff to be aware of this and make sure that behind the scenes is as tidy as it normally is. After all, you want candidates to go away with a good impression of the practice and they will tell others if what they see is untidy or dirty kennelling or prep area.

Interview preparation   Checklist

Candidates contacted and interview times arranged
Interviewers selected
Staff to show candidates around selected
Room booked
Seating arrangements
Refreshments
Receptionists given list of candidates and interview times
Interview questions set
Interview tests decided
Job description for each candidate
Personal profiles for each candidate
CVs and applications for each candidate
Interview assessment forms for each candidate

What documentation is needed?

All interviewers should have copies of the job description, personal profile and letter of application and CV or application form. They also need the candidate assessment form which they will be filling in at the end of the interview. They may also wish to have at hand any other information or documentation which relates to the job in case the candidate asks specific questions such as, 'Do you have health check forms?' or 'What sort of admissions form do you have?'

What questions will be asked?

Good and appropriate questioning of the candidate is vital. There are two main types of question, open and closed. It is important to ask mainly open questions, that is questions to which the candidate must give a considered and informative reply, and not closed questions to which they can just answer yes or no, as in these examples.

An open question – 'Tell me about your previous job responsibilities'.

A closed question – 'Did you enjoy your previous job?'

Open questions are designed to probe the candidate's knowledge, abilities and attitudes and to find out more about their character and

---

Figure 7   Interview questions

Here is just a small selection of general questions which could be used when interviewing veterinary, nursing and support staff. Clinical questions obviously depend on the practice concerned.

What attracted you to apply for this post?

Why do you want to change your present job?

How does this job fit in with your long-term career objectives?

We are looking to develop nursing clinics for our clients. How would you approach setting up a weight clinic in the practice?

Work in a veterinary practice is not always 9–5. How flexible can you be with your working hours?

What computer skills experience do you have?

What did/do you enjoy most about your previous/present job?

Describe the working relationship you have/had with your present/last employer.

What qualities do you possess that make you a good vet/receptionist/nurse?

What do you consider to be your greatest attributes?

What has been the highlight of your career so far?

What has been the low point of your career so far?

Why do you think it is important for clients to insure their pets?

What do you see as the main aims of a veterinary practice today?

Veterinary practices provide more services and sell more products than they used to. What sales and marketing skills do you have and how would you feel about promoting new products and services?

What experience have you of dealing with difficult or awkward clients?

What do you see as your main strengths both at and outside work?

We are able to provide increasingly more sophisticated treatment for pets, but at a financial cost to the client. Where do we draw the line?

How would you like to develop your interest in surgery?

What other interests or specialities do you have?

What is the secret to good teamwork?

What do you see as the role of veterinary support staff?

How do you see the veterinary profession in ten years time?

How do you see your role in the veterinary profession in five years time?

---

personality. Closed or specific questions are sometimes used when the interviewer needs facts or specific information, e.g. 'How long did you spend working in Australia?' Occasionally the candidate may be asked a leading question, e.g. 'Do you think that clients should be allowed to pay their bills by instalment?' and sometimes a hypothetical question such as 'Supposing a client's child started to get really noisy in the consulting room, what would you do?'

The majority of questions will be common to all candidates but there will be some individual questions based on their application forms/CVs and what they have listed as their hobbies and interests. These questions often tell you a great deal about the candidate's personality. Also try to anticipate candidate's questions so that you have answers ready which you all agree on. For example, what will you say if the candidate asks if the salary is negotiable or what the perks of the job are? Examples of some of the questions to ask at interviews are shown in figure 7.

If there is more than one person interviewing a candidate, allocate questions to each interviewer making sure they know the order in which the questions need to be asked. Clearly there may be some deviation from the plan, but it is important that the questioning session runs smoothly and this will only happen is everyone is prepared

Will there be psychometric testing of candidates?
Whether or not you carry out psychometric tests on candidates is entirely a matter of preference. Medium and larger sized businesses do often use some form of testing, indeed a survey by the Industrial Relations Services found that 83% of larger businesses in the UK use some form of psychometric testing when interviewing candidates. There are over 45 different companies producing such tests for sale, and in the UK in 1997 1.3 million of these tests were sold to businesses.

Employers use tests because they are held to be scientifically based and objective and can be very useful when combined with other interviewing techniques in identifying suitable people for specific jobs in an organisation. Whether or not psychometric testing is appropriate for selecting veterinary employees is a matter of debate, but it is useful to be aware of two of the main types of test available.

Personality tests
Personality tests assess and evaluate an individual's personality. They

help to predict how a person is likely to react under different circumstances. They measure attitude, habits and values. This type of test is not timed and you do not 'pass' or 'fail' it. Sometimes a test, or a particular section of it, is incorporated into an application form. This can be a very good idea if you are looking for a very specific personality.

Aptitude tests
Aptitude tests are an objective assessment of a candidate's ability; this may be their verbal understanding or their numeracy or logical reasoning. These tests are marked.

The subject of psychometric testing could fill a book all on its own and there are plenty of books around, as well as companies selling specialist tests. Such tests are not everyone's cup of tea and should be used carefully and with knowledge. Take care to use a reputable organisation for tests as they can be a potential minefield for the uninitiated.

To find out more details about psychometric testing you may wish to contact the following organisations:

British Psychological Society, St Andrew's House, 48 Princess Road East, Leicester LE1 7DR Tel 0116 254 9568   www.bps.org.uk
Institute of Personnel and Development, IPD House, 35 Camp Road, Wimbledon, London SW19 4UX Tel 020 8971 9000
www.ipd.co.uk
Department of Education and Skills, Sanctuary Buildings, Great Smith Street, London SW1 3ET.

How will the candidates be assessed?
An assessment form is one of the very best ways to assess a candidate. The form is in effect a revamping of the personal profile with boxes for comments or scoring. It enables all the interviewers to logically go through the criteria required, allocate scores or make comments and then compare the candidates. An assessment form helps the interviewer to remember which candidate was which – especially useful if you are interviewing quite a number of candidates over more than one day. Another important reason for having an assessment form is for record keeping and they should be kept for a minimum of six months, just in case a candidate decides to seriously query your reasons for not employing them. An example of an assessment form is shown in figure 8.

Interview structure   Checklist

Candidate arrives and waits in reception.
Member of staff shows the candidate around the practice for 20 minutes.
Same member of staff takes candidate to interview room.
Candidate is greeted and asked some informal questions to put them at
their ease.
Interviewers question candidate.
Candidate is asked if they have any questions.
Candidate is thanked for coming and shown back to the waiting room by
one of the interviewers.
Candidate told how they will hear the result of the interview.
If appropriate candidates' expenses are discussed/settled.
Candidate leaves.

The structure of the interview

Having considered the above areas it is important to plan the structure
of the interview itself, so that when the first candidate walks through
the interview room door, all the interviewers know exactly how the
interview will proceed. An example of an interview structure is shown
opposite.

What records will be kept?

Keep records relating to the interview for all those candidates interviewed both for the reason given above and also to refer to, in case
another post arises over the following few months. It may be that one
of the interviewees would fit this new position, if so you have all their
details to hand and this may avoid the costs of advertising. The records
you keep for the successful candidate will be useful at appraisal time
and should be kept together with other personal documentation in
their personal file.

Keep the following records:
◆ personal profile for the job
◆ job description
◆ the candidate's letter of application and C V or application form
◆ the list of questions asked
◆ the candidate's assessment form
◆ any other relevant material.

Summary

- Decide on the objectives of the interview.
- Good planning will ensure the interviewing is successful.
- Decide who is going to interview.
- It is a good idea to have another member of staff show the candidate around the practice, this will also act as an informal interview.
- Plan how long the interview will be and where it will be held.
- Make sure all the necessary staff know about the interviews.
- Prepare the documentation, decide on the questions to be asked and how candidates will be assessed.
- Plan the structure of the interview, having an interview checklist can be very helpful.
- Always keep records of the interview and the assessments made.

What the interviewers say

Q: How do you decide what questions to ask?

Denise – We now have standard questions for different members of staff. I decide what other questions to ask depending on what the applications are like and the information the candidates provide.

Mary – As well as general and more specific questions I also try to find questions to ask which arise as a result of the interview. It's a bit of thinking on your feet but sometimes the line of questioning is quite different from what you expected if a particular topic arises during the interview.

Q: Do you find it easy to organise the interview time?

Denise – It's not too bad, but it can be difficult if a candidate talks too much or too little.

Mary – It takes practice; the more you do it the easier it becomes. It is important not to over-run, but it's much worse when you feel you are running out of questions to ask and you just know that this isn't the right person for the job.

Q: Does it help to have all the interviews on the same day?

Mary – Yes, I hate it when it drags on for a few days with one or two interviewees each day. It makes it difficult to compare the candidates. It's also much better for the organisation of the practice and arranging to showing the candidates round and so on.

Denise – Yes, you can compare them all while they are all fresh in your mind.

Figure 8   Candidate assessment form

Post..................................

Name.. Date.................

Rating: 1 = poor 2 = average 3 = good 4 = very good

Assessment	Score 1–4	Comments
Personal qualities		
Personality		
Speech		
Bearing		
Manner		
Interpersonal skills		
Health and fitness		
Communication skills		
Flexibility		
Ability to fit in with staff		
Client-care skills		
Dependability		
Assertiveness		
Team member qualities		
Other qualities required		
Skills/experience		
Education		
Relevant experience		
Computer skills		
Numeracy		
Reception skills		
(If applicable)		
Nursing skills		
(If applicable)		
Clinical skills		
(If applicable)		
Other skills required		

Total score

Any other comments

Be aware that you may need to produce these assessment forms if any issue arises regarding the fairness of your selection, e.g. discrimination on grounds of disability, sex or race

7

Conducting the Interview

You have drawn up a job description, designed a personal profile, advertised the post, selected potential candidates for interview and prepared for the interviewing. This has all taken a considerable amount of time, now you have about forty-five minutes with each candidate in which to decide if they are the person for you. It's not a very long time so it is vital that you make the best use of the interview time.

There are three basic elements to interviewing – contact, content and control.

Contact and the building up of a rapport must be established at the outset of the interview or you will learn nothing from the candidate. Both the interviewer and interviewee need to be as relaxed as is possible in this artificial situation so that each manages to get from the interview the information they need.

The content of the interview is to a large extent the questions but it also means listening to candidates, probing further if questions are not answered satisfactorily, digesting information provided and answering candidates' questions. If the right questions are not asked the interview will end with the interviewer still not really knowing enough about the candidate and not being able to confidently make a judgement regarding their suitability.

The interviewer must always be in control of the interview. They should maintain the structure of the interview and not allow it to degenerate into a cosy chat just because they happen to be interested in one particular area of discussion. They should be able to steer the interview and the replies of the candidate in the right direction for further questioning and, very importantly, keep an eye on the time so that the interview is not in danger of over running.

None of this is easy but there is a logical order of play to an interview which, when followed, enables a smooth progression from meeting to parting with an efficient and effective exchange of information sandwiched in the middle. The steps of interviewing are described below and shown in the checklist.

Greeting the candidate and building rapport

Before any interview can effectively start the people present must build up some kind of rapport between themselves. When the candidate enters the interview room they should be welcomed, introduced to the interviewers and asked to take the seat indicated to them. Greet them in a friendly manner, smile – this always helps to break the ice and put a candidate at their ease.

⇨ Be positive – explain the interview procedure so that the candidate knows what to expect.

⇨ Be kind – provide a comforting environment as discussed in chapter 6.

⇨ Be interested – always try to show that you are interested in the candidate even if they are the last one of the day and you are desperate for a cup of tea.

First impressions

We are all susceptible to forming first impressions when we meet people and this is also the case when interviewing. There can be few of us who have not formed an immediate impression of someone before they have spoken or even looked in our direction. It is very important that we are aware of the effect first impressions can have. If we are not careful they can prejudice our judgement and slant an interview in the wrong direction. The formation of that first impression we have of someone is an intangible mix of the person's appearance, dress, manner, posture, body language and the general 'feel' they convey to us.

The rules we must obey as interviewers are:

⇨ To recognise our prejudices and overcome them.

⇨ Try to recognise the difference between someone who has not bothered to dress smartly for the interview, and someone who to us may look badly dressed but who, in fact, has taken a great deal of trouble to dress in what they consider to be a 'fashionable' style.

⇨ Remember that assumptions are not facts or evidence and we should base our judgements on the outcome of the interview.

The importance of body language

Body language plays an important part in communication between people and this is no less true of interviews. Posture and gestures count for more than 50% of non-verbal communication. The interviewer should aim to always give positive body language signals such as smiling open posture and good eye contact. Their objective is to put the candidate at their ease and encourage them to talk. This means you should not be fiddling with your pen, looking at your watch, sitting with your arms behind your head or stifling a yawn.

One of the first pieces of body language seen at the interview is the handshake. A warm dry firm handshake indicates a relaxed person, a limp, sweaty, 'wet fish' handshake suggests someone who is nervous and tense.

Look at the candidate's body language while they are talking, do the words they are saying match the actions they are displaying? Make a note of how good the candidate's eye contact is with the interviewers; good eye contact suggest a confident and honest personality while constantly looking down or away from the interviewer suggests timidity, nervousness and evasion. Think also how someone who never looks at the person they are talking to will come over to your clients, they are hardly going to be convincing in their diagnosis or explanations or treatment or healthcare. Body language is a whole science in itself. There are numerous interesting books on the subject that can certainly help you to understand better the physical actions displayed at interviews.

The way we think affects the way we communicate, if we can understand better how candidates are thinking we will be able to communicate better with them, by being on their 'wavelength'. If the interviewer can feed back some of the words the candidate uses to express the way they think, the candidate will feel on common ground and hopefully relax into the interview.

People have preferred styles of communication which can be separated into three main types, visual, auditory and kinaesthetic.

Visual style

These people think in pictures. When remembering events they describe how things looked, when they are thinking about ideas and plans they think of the big picture not the little details. The words they use will give you clues; they will say such things as:

'That looks good'
'I see what you mean'
'I get the picture'.

These people tend to look up to the right when constructing thoughts and up to the left when providing information. They often speak quite quickly and use exaggerated gestures

Auditory style

These people think in sounds. They remember detail and usually give very detailed answers to questions. They will use phrases such as:

'I hear what you say'
'That sounds good'
'In a manner of speaking'.

Their lips will often move as they read, they will have rhythmic body movements and may have a voice with a good tonal range. Their eye movements are from side to side; they will look towards their right ear when constructing information and towards their left ear when recalling events.

Kinaesthetic style

These people think in feelings. They will go into great depth when describing events and tend to be slower of speech. They will use phrases such as:

'How does that feel?'
'I can't put my finger on it'
'We need to dig deeper into this'.

Kinaesthetic people tend to display minimal gestures and often pause in their speech. They will look down to the right when constructing thoughts and down to the left when recalling events

When building your rapport with candidates it is extremely helpful to be aware of these communication preferences so that you can communicate effectively. So faced with a visual candidate you will be asking them how they see their career developing over the next five years, not how do they feel their career will develop over the next five years. And if you are talking to a kinaesthetic person you will need to speak rather more slowly and not rush them into answering.

Good interviewing   Checklist

Before the interview
Prepare the interview room
Have all documentation at hand
Inform all relevant staff
Re-read the candidates' applications

The interview
Introduce the interviewers
Put candidates at ease
Start the interview slowly
Provide background information
Start questioning on familiar ground
Ask open questions
Encourage candidate to speak freely
Avoid personal prejudices and discrimination
Make sure full terms of employment are explained
Keep to time
Take notes
Inform candidate when they are likely to hear from you
Thank candidate for attending

After the interview
Have time to discuss each candidate
Be objective
Complete assessment forms
Ask for opinions from other staff members

Asking questions

Unless you want a very specific answer, ask open questions which allow the candidate to give full replies. A list of typical questions was given at the end of chapter 6. You will have worked out before hand who will be asking the different questions, but be prepared to deviate from the plan if it means you will have a better interview and find out more about the candidate.

Ask the questions in a logical sequence. It can be confusing to jump around from 'Tell me about the responsibilities you had in your last job' to 'Where did you go on your holidays last year?' and then back to 'What would you do if a client started to shout at you in the reception area?'

Link your questions to the candidate's replies and pursue particular lines of enquiry if you think they will be helpful in assessing the candidate. Probe for answers if you feel that the candidate's reply was too superficial or guarded.

Don't be afraid of silences, they provide thinking time for both you and the candidate. Note how the candidate responds to the silence, do they rush to fill it or have they the confidence to take their time and think of the answer they wish to give.

Avoid multiple or ambiguous questions such as 'Do you think clients should be allowed to pay their bills in instalments and how would you deal with someone who said they had left their purse at home?' or 'Some people think that nurses these days are becoming over-qualified for their roles in practice; would you like to study for a diploma when you are more experienced?'

Don't interrupt the candidate when they are talking if it is just to give your own opinion or you don't agree with what they are saying, and don't argue with them or criticise. This behaviour is simply not appropriate at an interview, and really it is not important if you do not agree with them when you will not be employing them. The important thing is for them to leave with a good impression of you and the practice, not to go home and tell everyone in the pub that night what an argumentative vet or manager they have at the practice down the road.

Always try to look interested in what the candidate is saying even if you are not. There is nothing worse for an interviewee than it being patently obvious that they are boring the pants off the interviewers. How can they possibly show themselves at their best under

such circumstances?

When you have completed your questioning, ask the candidate if they have any questions. Most will have some ready that they 'prepared earlier' but if they seem to be struggling help them along a little by asking, for example, if there is anything more you can tell them about the duty rota. Or if they seemed particularly interested or concerned about a particular matter ask if they would like further information.

Listening

The importance of listening cannot be stressed enough. It is only by listening that the interviewer will really get to know the facts about the candidate and be able to form a true picture of them. This is why is it is important that you let the candidate do the talking – so that you can do the listening. Generally speaking you should aim to allow the candidate to do 75%–80% of the talking. The more the candidate talks the more information you are gleaning about them.

Think about the actual language they use and how eloquent they are at expressing themselves and conveying information. Remember that they may be dealing all day with clients and they need to be good communicators. Listen to the tone of the voice and the way things are said. Is it a gentle reassuring voice or harsh and aggressive, do they speak clearly or mumble? How will a client hear this voice in the consulting room or waiting room?

Listen also, because some candidates will trip themselves up if they talk long enough. They may contradict themselves, or perhaps start to tell you something that they later wish they hadn't. If a candidate starts to criticise their old practice for example or be indiscreet about clients they have dealt with, consider whether they will be doing the same in your practice in a few months time if you appoint them.

Controlling the interview

You, the interviewer, must be in control of the interview 100% of the time.

Interviews can get horribly out of hand if there is a combination of a very assertive or dominant candidate and an inexperienced interviewer. Do not allow the candidate to take over and dominate the interview, steering it in the direction they want and talking about the topics they wish to talk about. Don't allow the candidate to start asking all the questions and, in effect, interview you.

Controlling the interview also means keeping a careful check on the time and working your way through the interview at a measured and organised pace. So that at the end of the 45 minutes you have also come to the end of the interview and are not only half way through it.

Control of the interview comes with experience but there are a number of actions which can help.

⇨ If the candidate is talking too much, politely cut short responses with 'I see, so...' or, 'That's interesting, let's move on now to...'

⇨ Be prepared to allocate time to each question and keep a careful eye on the time. Don't of course keep looking at your watch, much better to have it lying on the table where you can glance at it without it being too obvious to the candidate.

⇨ Talk to any colleague who is interviewing with you and plan how you will conduct the interview. If necessary try a dry run to test out the timing.

⇨ Be prepared for the candidate who talks very little, in this case you may have too much time for the interview. Have some reserve questions up your sleeve.

⇨ Resist the temptation to get too involved in a question or in talking to the candidate, at the risk of not asking the more important questions.

Holidays and periods of notice

Do not forget to ask candidates if they have holiday already booked. This should not affect your final decision but it is important for planning to know at this stage if they will be absent from work. The period of notice they are required to give should also be established. If you desperately need a replacement employee, someone who has to give three months notice may not be an option for recruitment. However at the same time, don't appoint someone just because they can 'start tomorrow' thereby getting you out of a 'hole'. If they find it so easy to leave their present job, will they find it just as easy to leave this one?

References

It is always helpful to have references for a candidate but they should be used with care mainly to confirm factual information. Referees are increasingly reticent about giving too much personal information for fear of appearing to be defamatory. Providing an outline of the job for the potential referee enables them to give you a fair assessment of how they think the candidate from their own experience will be able to handle the role. Always remember to obtain the applicant's consent to taking up referees and be wary of any applicant who is unable to provide any reference names – ask yourself, why not?

On 1st April 2002 the Criminal Records Bureau (CRB) was launched. This is a new disclosure service aimed at protecting children and young people from violence and abuse. The CRB allows prospective employers to check potential applicants in order to identify people who may be unsuitable to work in areas involving contact with children, young people or vulnerable adults. More information about this service and its use can be provided by the CRB whose details are given in the appendix of useful addresses. Although testimonials are often provided with a candidates CV, employers should also seek confidential references and not rely on testimonials alone.

Closing the interview

At the end of the interview there are a number of formalities which should be completed. Thank the interviewee for attending, offer them the opportunity to telephone the practice if there are further questions they want answered. Give some indication of the length of time they may have to wait before hearing the result of the interview and assure them that they will receive notification even if they are not successful.

Wish the candidate goodbye and show them from the interview room back into the waiting room. Do not just leave them to find their own way out of the practice. At this stage it is also appropriate to sort out any expenses the candidate may have if it is the practice policy to reimburse the candidates with travelling costs, etc. Make sure the candidates leave the practice with a good impression.

Assessing the candidates

Before the next candidate is interviewed, the interviewers should complete the assessment form and discuss the last candidate. It is vital to record this information and your impressions before you go on to interview someone else and the personalities merge. Use the assessment form to score the candidate or simply comment on the qualities listed. Once all the interviewing is completed a full comparison of candidates can then more easily be made.

Discrimination

Lack of planning or thought can entangle interviewers in discriminatory behaviour. Whether discrimination is active or accidental the consequences can be serious and potentially costly.

Active discrimination

Advertising for male- or female-only employees, candidates of a particular race or religion, people under the age of 35 or asking either male or female candidates how soon they intend to start a family are clearly discriminatory and have to be avoided. Questions at interviews and the wording of adverts must always be politically correct, if there are ever any doubts legal advice should be sought. Once you have all your interviewing and selection paperwork prepared, it may be advisable to ask a legal expert to check it over for any breaches of discrimination legislation.

Accidental/unintentional discrimination

This sort of discrimination is less easy to qualify and deserves more comment. These types of discrimination take a number of different forms.

◆ Unequal treatment at interview, for example giving one candidate 20 minutes and another 40 minutes could allow a candidate to complain of discrimination on the grounds of time.

◆ If you do not use basically the same broad band of questions with each candidate, discrimination might occur.

◆ The mind of the interviewer may already before the interview be discriminating against a candidate. We all have names we don't like because of memories of conflict with people of that name, so if an applicant's name is Peter and the interviewer has a real problem with this the applicant may get no further than the reject pile.

◆ We build up pictures in our mind of a candidate from reading their CV, often to be disappointed when we meet them in the flesh. Likewise first impressions can be difficult to remove from our minds.

◆ Ageism can unconsciously affect our judgement simply by us thinking that we want someone younger for the job or someone more mature so that they can 'deal better' with clients.

◆ Psychometric tests must also be devised to be fair and relevant for the position being advertised, and should not be biased towards

gender or culture.
◆ Then there are the stereotypical candidates, the 'do-gooder' or the 'social climber' and we all must have come across the 'I've always wanted to work with animals, they are my life' applicant. We immediately pigeonhole these people, sometimes at the expense of really listening to them to find out what they are actually like and how good they would be at the job we are interviewing them for.
◆ Beware of physical characteristics and the assumption we sometimes make about them, e.g. people with red hair are quick tempered, people with eyes that are close together can't be trusted.
◆ Also beware of the 'halo effect', where one feature of the candidate becomes an overriding factor and governs our perception of the person. For example they may be exceptionally pretty, or have an appalling dress sense, have a very seductive voice or be very good at one particular veterinary skill.

All these areas could be possible discriminatory pitfalls and this is why the interview should be so carefully thought out, questions devised and objectivity maintained as far as possible.

Why interviews fail

This is very simple. Interviews fail for two main reasons.

1 Lack of preparation

Interviews do not just happen, they have to be designed and organised as we have already discussed. Asking someone to just turn up for a chat to see if they fancy the job or if they will be OK to fill the post is a recipe for disaster. You must know who you are looking for and be able to recognise when you have found them.

Lack of preparation works both ways. What is a potential employee going to think if they arrive at the practice for an interview and you only manage to spare them ten minutes between operations, or keep them waiting half an hour while you attend to other matters or finish consulting? This is not a good advertisement for the organisation of the practice and the candidate may well think twice before accepting a job working there.

2 Lack of interviewer training

We have said already that interviewing is not easy. Not everyone is good at it or enjoys it, and no one will be successful without at least some basic training in interviewing skills. It really is worth sending any potential interviewer on an interview skills course to give them the basic skills of interviewing. A badly conducted interview results in a badly selected employee or possibly the loss of a potentially good employee.

Summary

- The interviewer must always remain in control of the interview.
- It is important to build up a good rapport with the candidates from the very beginning of the interview.
- Be aware of body language but be careful not to read too much into it.
- Be very careful about making decisions based only on first impressions.
- Try to communicate with candidates in the style they understand best, i.e. visual, auditory and kinaesthetic.
- Ask open questions unless you require a very specific answer.
- Pursue any loopholes, discrepancies or queries seen in the job application form or CV.
- Listen carefully to the answers the candidates give.
- Always follow up a candidate's references.
- Always try to tell the candidate when you expect to be able to let them know if they have been successful or not.
- Avoid discrimination when interviewing candidates.
- Interviews are unsuccessful because of lack of preparation and poor interviewing techniques.

What the interviewers say

Q: Do you enjoy interviewing?

Denise – Yes, especially now I do more and feel more confident about it.

Mary – Yes, actually I enjoy meeting the people. It's not easy and sometimes when you know you have selected the wrong person to interview it can be frustrating, but I do look forward to the days when I am interviewing.

Q: How do you cope with 'first impressions'?

Mary – You are bound to be affected by the first impression so I try to accept it, put it to the back of my mind and get on with the interview. But you have to remember that it's something like this first impression that a client may get, so in fact it does have a bearing on the final selection.

Denise – It's very difficult, the first impression of a person does tend to stick and sometimes it can definitely be the wrong one. You just have to try hard to be objective.

Q: Is it easy to improvise questions?

Denise – It depends on the candidate and what they say but if they are quite talkative it is fairly easy to pick up on things they say and ask more questions about them.

Mary – It gets a lot easier with experience. Now I don't find it difficult. You have to listen carefully to what is being said and pick up on any points of interest.

Q: How do you get the best from the candidate?

Denise – Make sure they are relaxed, and be friendly. But you have to be professional and organised so that they are left with a good impression.

Mary – You have to be relaxed and confident as an interviewer. Explain how the interview will be carried out and be friendly but not too 'chatty' or they will be confused and get mixed messages.

Q: How do you assess the candidates on dress, punctuality and nerves?

Denise – Dress does make a difference to me, I am more impressed if someone looks smart. You have to look beyond the nervousness, but if they are excessively nervous you have to think how they will cope with dealing with clients etc. I don't like it if they are late, it gives a bad impression.

Mary – The style of dress does not matter to me too much as long as I can see that they have made an effort. I do take nerves into account when assessing candidates but sometimes it can be difficult to distinguish nervousness from manner or attitude. Being late receives a 'black mark' unless they have contacted us to warn us and given a good reason.

8

Decision Time

The interviews are over and now it is decision time. Throughout the recruiting and selection process your aim has been to identify the candidates most suitable for the job you have on offer. At the end of interviewing you have some very detailed information on a number of selected candidates and it is from these few that the final choice must be made.

The final assessment

Assessing and comparing the interviewed candidates should be done as soon as possible after the interviewing has been completed, while all the candidates are fresh in the minds of the interviewers. There are three main ways of carrying out this final assessment:

◆ completed assessment forms and notes
◆ personal opinions and feelings
◆ staff opinion.

Completed assessment forms and notes

The interviewing team should have already completed an interview assessment form for each candidate. They should now spend some time looking again at the forms and comparing candidates. Remember to check any other notes you may have made about the candidate during the interview. Did they make eye contact, did they mumble, was there anything that upset you or that you disliked? Or did you perhaps just make a note that they were a really friendly person, easy to get on with or very open. It may be these apparently small details which could make all the difference in choosing. Some candidates may have been rejected and there may be one who stands out from the others, if this is the case the job is easy.

However, often there will be a number of candidates from whom it is quite difficult to choose. Consider which candidate fits the original specification the best. Will they fit in with the practice, its culture and its staff and clients and will the practice suit them? It does not matter how well the candidate fits the technical or managerial skills required if their people skills are poor. The success of a veterinary practice today is based very largely on its people skills, if they are lacking, the practice will flounder. So don't make a rod for your back by employing a new member of staff who is not going to communicate or relate well with staff or clientele.

If, after discussing the candidates, you still cannot make a final decision between the last two or three it may be wise to call them back for a second interview. This interview may be with one different interviewer so that a fresh viewpoint can help on the final decision. Likewise, even if you think you know which candidate you want but there are still one or two niggling doubts – however small – invite them back; if they really want the job they will be happy to return for a second interview.

Some practices invite the final two or three candidates to the practice for a few days to work and meet potential colleagues, so that more members of staff have a chance to talk and work with them. This allows the candidate to make a more informed decision on whether the job and the practice are for them and allows you to decide if the candidate is for the practice. Although this can work well it is of course often difficult for candidates to take time off from their existing jobs at short notice.

Personal opinions and feelings

Although you have to be very careful to avoid bias and discrimination when it comes to personal feelings, there is no doubt that we all at some time simply have the feeling that this is just not the person we want to employ. We are unable to put our finger on exactly what we are unhappy about but we 'just know' there is something not quite right. We should not ignore these feelings but we should try to discuss them with others to see if they also have any reservations.

In this instance, calling the person back for a second interview to see if these first impressions remain could be very helpful. This time round the feelings may have gone (or they could be even stronger) either way you have achieved the result you wanted, and are able to more easily make a decision. If you feel very strongly on the matter, it should be taken into consideration when making the final choice especially if one of the interviewers has to work closely with the person.

Staff opinion

Listen to what your staff say. Some of your staff will have met the candidates as they were being shown around, the candidate's guide will have had a chance to talk to them while showing them the practice. Ask this member of staff and any others who met the candidates what they thought. Ask them if they would be happy working with them. If you receive an overwhelming 'no' think very, very carefully before offering the candidate the job. It is your staff who will be working with this new person, often very closely and in small teams. You do not want any more conflict or difficulties than you may have already so don't make even more problems for yourself and the practice.

Capability versus suitability

Below are two case studies illustrating the importance of balancing capability and suitability in potential employees.

Case 1

Mary is interviewed for a receptionist's role by the practice manager and head receptionist. Both feel that Mary would be ideal for the job, she has good people skills an apparently friendly and open manner and seems very capable. However when staff are asked their views, the main full–time receptionist and two part-timers say that they really do not think that there is any way that they could work with Mary. Of course, their reasons must be carefully probed to ensure that discrimination is not one of their reasons. The new recruit would have to work very closely with the other receptionists, they would provide cover for each other and spend a lot of time working side by side.

Decision – Don't employ Mary

Reasons

We have a very good reception team, by employing Mary even though she has the potential to make a good receptionist we would disrupt the working of the existing team.

Case 2

Sue is a three-year qualified veterinary surgeon. We are looking for an experienced vet who can take responsibility and help run our branch practice. Sue has no real experience of independent working other than of course being on duty. However she has a lovely personality, got on well with the staff when she came to 'see' practice for three days and even in that short space of time we had clients commenting on how pleasant she was. She seems to have really good people skills.

Decision – Employ Sue

Reasons

She may not yet have enough experience to help run the branch surgery but her other qualities outweigh this. She will become an excellent and valuable team member and help provide good client care and bonding. We can continue to run the branch practice as we have done for a little longer and deploy one of the other vets in this area, while planning Sue's training so that she will eventually fit into this particular role.

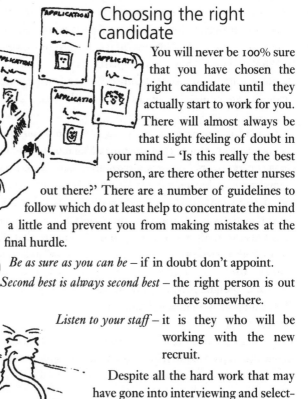

Choosing the right candidate

You will never be 100% sure that you have chosen the right candidate until they actually start to work for you. There will almost always be that slight feeling of doubt in your mind – 'Is this really the best person, are there other better nurses out there?' There are a number of guidelines to follow which do at least help to concentrate the mind a little and prevent you from making mistakes at the final hurdle.

Be as sure as you can be – if in doubt don't appoint.

Second best is always second best – the right person is out there somewhere.

Listen to your staff – it is they who will be working with the new recruit.

Despite all the hard work that may have gone into interviewing and selecting it is still better to cut one's losses and start again, if you are not as sure as it is possible to be that this is the right person for the job. Although expensive in the short term, taking on a locum until the post has been filled may be a cheaper option than recruiting the wrong person.

Even if the interviewers think they have found the right person they should listen very carefully to what the staff think about the candidate. It is these staff who will be working with them on a day-to-day basis and if they simply cannot get on with the rest of the staff, it doesn't matter how good a vet, nurse or receptionist they are.

The job offer

Once you have made your decision, act quickly. If you think you have found a really good vet or nurse for your practice then it is very likely that so will the other practices the nurse or vet has applied to.

It is sensible to telephone the person with the initial offer to find out if they are still interested in the post. If they are, follow up straight away with the offer letter. This letter formally offers the job to the candidate and should contain at least the following information.

- ◆ Title of post
- ◆ Starting date, time and place
- ◆ Salary and other benefits
- ◆ Contract of employment
  Ideally, the contract of employment should be sent with the job offer. This allows the potential employee to read it through and discuss areas of concern before the appointment is made. There can be nothing worse than appointing, for example, a vet for whom you have waited two or three months only to find that once they have started work and are given their contract, they do not want to sign it because of clauses they do not wish to comply with. Far better to have the contract signed and sealed before the employee starts work.
- ◆ Housing details if accommodation is supplied by the practice.
- ◆ Local information about houses to buy or rent if the person is to find their own accommodation.
- ◆ Uniform
  The practice will need to know the person's size so that uniforms can be ordered.
- ◆ Equipment which will be supplied
- ◆ Car details if the practice supplies a car

◆ Car parking facilities
  Better to inform the new member of staff where they are expected
  to park their car than find that on their first morning they have
  parked in the senior partner's space!
  Always request written confirmation of the job acceptance by a set
time e.g. 'Please confirm your acceptance of this post in writing by...'
  Do not send letters of rejection to the other interviewees until you have
acceptance in writing from the chosen candidate. You may have a second
person who you would offer the job to, were your first choice to have
already accepted another post or decided they don't want your job after all.

The unsuccessful candidates

Always reply to every applicant. One of the commonest complaints
from job seekers is that they never receive replies to their job applications. At the simplest level this is just impolite on the part of the
organisation. We talked about creating an impression of the practice on
the candidates; if you fail to reply to applications, or worse interviewees, you will not create a very good impression of the organisation of
the practice or its client care.

If you have not already informed those applicants who did not
receive interviews that they have been unsuccessful this should be done
straight away. A very simple letter is sufficient, thanking them for
applying but informing them that they have not been successful.

A different letter needs to be sent to those candidates who were

---

Figure 9   **Sample rejection letter: non-
                                             interviewees**

Title of post

Address

Date

Dear ....
Thank you for applying for the above position.
Unfortunately you have not been successful in your application, but we wish
you success in finding a suitable post in the near future.
Yours sincerely

Name...........................
Practice Manager

Figure 10   Sample rejection letter: interviewees

Title of post

Address

Date

Dear ....
Thank you for applying for attending for interview for the above position.
The standard of candidates was extremely high and it was not easy to make
our final choice. We have however offered the position to one of the other
candidates who has accepted our offer.
It was a pleasure to meet you and interview you and we would like to wish
you success in finding a suitable job in the very near future.
Yours sincerely

Name...........................
Practice Manager

---

interviewed. In some cases it will have been difficult to choose between the candidates, this should be reflected in the tone of the rejection letter. 'The standard of interviewees was very high' or 'We had difficulty choosing from the high standard of candidates we interviewed' will indicate that the interviewee performed well.

It may be appropriate in some cases to explain why they were not offered the job, 'We were looking for someone with more computer skills', or 'We were looking for someone who had more experience leading a nursing team'. It is always useful for a candidate to know why they did not get the job, and for them to know when appropriate that they interviewed well, made no mistakes but simply weren't the right person for the job.

Unsuccessful interviewees will occasionally telephone the practice to enquire why they were not offered the job, it is much better to have put this in writing than be put on the spot on the telephone. However as always when giving the explanation for rejection be careful to avoid any discriminatory language or inferences.

You may wish to keep candidates' letters on file if you were impressed by them and think that if a different job became available they may be suitable. If this is the case ask the candidate if this is acceptable to them. It is good to end the letter by wishing them success in their job hunting, 'We wish you well in your future career', or 'We hope you are successful in finding a post in the near future'.

Figure 11   Sample acceptance letter

Title of post

Address1

Date

Dear ....
Thank you for attending for interview for the above position. We are pleased to be able to offer you the position at a salary of.............. Your working hours will be.............
Two copies of your contract of employment are enclosed. Please sign one and return it with your letter of acceptance and keep the other for your own records.
Your starting date will be...... Please report to the Practice Manager on arrival, when you will be given other relevant documentation.
We will be contacting you regarding your first two weeks induction timetable and uniform/clothing requirements in the near future.
We would be pleased to receive your confirmation in writing that you wish to accept this position by.........
If you have any queries between now and beginning your employment with us please do not hesitate to contact ....
We are looking forward to you joining our Practice team.
Yours sincerely

Name...........................
Practice Manager

Summary

- Assess and compare the candidates as soon as possible after the interviewing.
- Use assessment forms to score candidates and compare their total marks.
- Call candidates back for a second interview if a final decision cannot be make after the first interview.
- Seek the opinions of staff, they are the ones who will have to work with the new employee.
- Avoid personal feelings prejudicing your choice of candidate.
- Avoid discrimination.
- If you are not sure do not appoint.
- Make the job offer as soon as possible in case your chosen candidate is offered a job by another practice.

- A job offer by phone followed up by the formal job offer letter will speed up the process.
- Make sure all the necessary information is included in the job offer letter.
- It is good practice to send the job contract before the employee starts work so that no problems regarding employment arise after they have accepted the job.
- Always reply to all the unsuccessful candidates, this will help to maintain the good image of the practice.

What the interviewers say

Q: How do you make the final choice?

Denise – Sometimes it is really easy and the person we want stands out a mile. We use an assessment form and this helps to confirm this sort of candidate as well as make choosing from similar ones more easy.

Mary – It's often not easy especially when you have two or three who would all be good at the job. Then we often go on the staff's comments and how they think they would fit into the practice. It's wonderful when there is one person who you just know is the 'right one for the job'. The assessment form is very helpful, it helps you to remember candidates and compare them. We score them, which is also helpful when making the final assessment.

Q: Do you rely on your 'gut' feelings when deciding?

Denise – Yes. A lot, and I am almost always right.

Mary – Yes, but I try to be rational about it and look at all the other factors. But at the end of the day if there are two candidates and we have explored everyone's opinions and we still can't decide it has to come down to that gut feeling.

Q: Do you listen to staff opinion?

Denise – Yes, but it does depend to some extent on who the staff member is. If they are a more 'difficult' staff member, I may not take as much notice of their opinion.

Mary – Yes, it's important to listen to staff especially if they will be working directly with the new employee.

9

Being an Interviewee

So you've been asked for interview. This means that you are probably one of four to six people who have been selected as possible new recruits. This is the moment to be really positive. Your chances of getting this job have now been seriously increased from perhaps 5% to at the very least 25%. There is a one-in-four chance that you will be successful not a four-to-one chance that you will be unsuccessful.

You must now concentrate your mind on why you are the right person for the job. You will only have been called for interview if the selectors think you can do the job. The purpose of the interview is to find out more about you, your personality, people skills, attitude, ambitions and dreams for the future. The secret to interviewing well is being prepared. This takes time but it is time well spent.

Be prepared
The practice
It is important to find out as much as possible about the practice. You will not impress the interviewers if they realise you have no idea about the practice, the work it does or how many staff are employed. Look at the practice website and brochure. If you live locally you may already use the practice as a client, but it is always worth asking other clients about the practice if this is possible. It is very useful to have an 'outsider's' opinion on the organisation you may be working for. Great if the response to 'What do you think of .... Veterinary Surgery' is positive, but if the reply is 'Very expensive and not very helpful' you may need to think carefully about your next move.

You may even consider visiting the surgery, perhaps to talk to the practice manager about the job, or maybe phone for more information. Plan how you will get to the interview: have you been sent a map, how far away is it? How long will it take to drive there, how much time do you need to give yourself? It is a cardinal sin to be late for an interview.

The job
Find out as much as you can about the job. Read the job description in detail; if you have not been sent one, phone and ask for more details. The interviewers are going to ask you why you should be given the job, so you need to have the answer. Decide what you have that makes you special and what benefits there will be from employing you. List the skills and experience you will bring to the post. Think about what you are good at, what you have achieved, the areas both at work and outside that you are proud of, and all your good qualities.

You are selling yourself at the interview, so you need to be positive and know exactly why you should have the job. If you think you can't do something or won't achieve a goal the likelihood is that you are right. It is the same with an interview, if you go into it expecting to be rejected you will be.

The interview process
Try to find out how the interview will be conducted, how long it will be, if there are second interviews, if you will be shown around, etc. This all helps you to prepare and know what to expect.

The questions you will be asked
Anticipate the questions that you may be asked and have answers to them. These questions are often the commonest.
◆ Tell me about yourself.
◆ Tell me about your last job.
◆ What makes you the best person for this post?
◆ What qualities will you bring to the job?
◆ Why do you want to leave your present job?
◆ What did you enjoy most about your last job?
◆ What are your strengths?
◆ What are your weaknesses?
Be able to answer these questions. There will be others that you may not anticipate but at least if you have a ready answer for some the

pressure will be eased and your comfort zone will be greater. Practice the answers with a friend acting as the interviewer.

What questions will you ask?

You will almost certainly be asked if you have any questions. Have some ready. Often many of the questions you have prepared are answered during the course of the interview, so rather than have to say 'I think you have answered all my questions' think of one or two such as 'What is the expansion plan for the practice over the next ten years?' or 'What is the practice feeling on expanding nursing clinics or having specialist clinics in ....?'

It is important not to ask some particular questions at this stage of the interview. Do not ask as your only question 'How much sick pay does the practice pay?' or 'Can I bring my dog to work with me?' or 'Can I take holidays on my duty weekends?' Such housekeeping questions may well need to be asked but if done at this stage may well not endear you to the interviewers.

References

If you have not already given the names of two referees on your CV or application form, have names ready at the interview. Make sure you have all contact details. Appearing hesitant about naming referees can look suspicious and will worry the interviewer.

Dress

Dress is often seen as a contentious issue. There are two main schools of thought.
1 They can take me as they find me – clothes do not matter – it's how good I will be at the job that is important.
2 Wearing the 'right' clothes will impress the interviewers and show that I am interested in the job.

Both statements can be justified but it is highly likely that an interviewer will look on the person who follows the second statement far more favourably.

In the eyes of most interviewers dress makes a statement about the interviewee. A well-groomed and well-dressed person is usually perceived to be a better prospect for employment. Many interviewers may not themselves care too much about how a person dresses but certainly in a veterinary practice they must consider the feelings and attitudes of their clients.

For most clients a smartly dressed member of staff or vet says a 'smartly' or well-run practice. A scruffily dressed or badly groomed individual, especially a receptionist (the first person most clients meet), says a scruffily run practice. If they care so little about their appearance how much will they care about the work they do? These may be totally unfair comments but this can be the perception of the client.

If gaining a job that you really want means making a relatively small effort to look smart and wear a suit or your 'Sunday best' then surely it is worth the trouble.

There are some basic rules about dressing for interviews.

⇨ Look smart, clean and tidy.
⇨ For women, wear a suit or smart skirt/trousers and jacket.
⇨ For men, wear a suit or smart trousers and jacket.
⇨ Wear clothes that are comfortable so that they don't cause added anxiety at the interview.
⇨ Do not wear 'high fashion' clothes keep these for the disco or club!
⇨ Have tidy, clean hair.
⇨ Wear clean shoes.

The issue of ordinary jewellery and body-piercing jewellery is important in veterinary practice both from a hygiene and health-and-safety point of view. Many practices will insist on nurses wearing no jewellery while working and may feel unhappy about a receptionist who has visible body piercing. If you go to an interview with nose, eyebrow or tongue jewellery, their removal for work may be a part of the conditions of employment.

Manner and body language
Interviewers gain a lot of information from non-verbal communication, most of which is

the body language of the interviewee.

Sometimes their very first impression is from the greeting hand-shake, and what can be more off putting than the so-called 'wet fish' handshake? This is the limp, lifeless, slightly damp hand proffered by the interviewee which sends a little shudder down the spine. Although no one will be turned down just on their handshake it does not get the interview off to a very good start if you are one of these wet fish. The handshake should be firm and positive but not a 'bone crusher' – this is not an arm wrestling competition.

It is important to smile and maintain reasonable eye contact with the interviewers, without of course staring them out. Show you are listening by nodding and leaning forward in your chair.

Sit comfortably, not on the edge of the chair as this makes you look anxious. Place the legs in the low-cross position, i.e. ankles crossed and rest your hands on your thighs. Do not fidget with your hands, this is both distracting and annoying to others.

The day of the interview

Have an interview checklist like the one above to make sure you have all the information you need for the interview.

Give yourself plenty of time to get to the interview. If you are held up for any reason, phone the practice and explain that you will be late, giving an estimated time of arrival. They will understand if your train is delayed or you are stuck in a traffic jam, but not if you just turn up half an hour late for the interview.

The interview starts the moment you arrive in the car park and ends

---

Interviewee preparation   **Checklist**

What do I know about the practice?
Do I know how to get there?
What do I need to know about the job?
How will the interview be conducted, are there second interviews?
What questions am I likely to be asked?
What questions do I want to ask?
Why do I want the job?
Why should I be given the job?
What benefits will I bring to the practice?
What are my long-term ambitions?
What are my strengths and weaknesses
What will I wear?

---

only as you drive away. Every moment you are there you are being interviewed in some way, whether it is by the receptionist who greets you (and who is later asked by the interviewers how you introduced yourself), the nurse or vet who showed you round, or the member of staff you talked to in the loo. Do not be caught off your guard. Interviewers learn a great deal about the interviewee outside the interview room.

Arrive early, this allows you time to compose yourself, use the loo, read the handouts and displays in the waiting room and generally soak in the atmosphere. Watch the staff, see how they treat the clients, how they behave and dress; this will tell you a great deal about the practice and its culture.

Use all this information in the interview if you have the opportunity. It will show the interviewers that you are observant and interested in the practice and how it is run.

At the interview
This is your chance to impress and show why you are the right person for the job.

Take the opportunity of open questions to tell the interviewers as much as you can. Show them that you have the experience and the knowledge to do the job. Show that you are motivated and in particular show that you have good communication skills – something particularly important for those working in veterinary practice. Try to show how you get on with others and how you work as a team member. Explain the benefits you will bring to the practice, it may be your experience in management, the behaviour qualification you have, you may be a certificate holder or have a lot of experience in holding puppy parties. Whatever your skills are, show how the practice will benefit from employing them.

Be assertive, using phrases such as 'I can' rather than 'I think I can.' Do not be too modest about your abilities but do be careful not to sound too big headed. Use phrases like 'friends tell me that I am a very good communicator' or 'my employer said I was a very good team member'.

When you are being asked questions always stop to ask yourself:
1 Why are they asking me this?
2 What is the best answer I can give?
3 How shall I reply?

Figure 12   **The Do's and Don'ts guide for interviewees**

DO
   Think before you speak
   Smile
   Make eye contact
   Be aware of body language
   Have questions to ask
   Look interested
   Listen
   Dress smartly
DON'T
   Lie
   Joke
   Argue
   Eat or smoke
   Interrogate the interviewer
   Take over the interview
   Be too familiar
   Criticise your last employer or comment indiscreetly on their business

---

Take a little time to answer, get your brain in gear rather than leaping into the reply without thinking and then finding you are digging a very big hole for yourself.

⇨ Keep positive. A negative reply such as 'I didn't enjoy that part of the job' will prompt another question. Saying, 'I enjoyed this part the best' may be a better reply.

⇨ Don't be too chatty or familiar, even if it is a fairly informal interview and don't make jokes. Never eat or chew gum or smoke unless invited to do so.

⇨ Even if you don't agree with something the interviewers say do not get into an argument, this will not increase your chances of being offered the job.

⇨ Never, ever lie about your qualifications or experience; a good interviewer will check references and eventually you will be exposed.

⇨ Be prepared for the 'strengths and weaknesses' question and remember that weaknesses are not necessarily bad. What the interviewer wants to know is whether or not you are aware of them and what you do to overcome them.

⇒ Have your own questions ready. Don't have too many and don't make it an interrogation. Be careful not to ask only housekeeping questions such as 'How much sick pay do you give?' or 'How much time off in lieu will you give for attending out-of-hours meetings'. These are the sort of questions that start alarm bells ringing for the interviewers.

⇒ At the end of the interview be sure you know what happens next. If you are not told, ask when you are likely to hear if you have been successful or will be called for a second interview. Do not leave with uncertainties in your mind

You are likely to be asked how much notice you need to give your present employer and if you have any holidays booked for the current year. Try to have this information available it is helpful to the interviewers and looks more organised on your part than having to say you will let them know

For a quick guide to the 'do's and don'ts' for interviewees see figure 12. The interviewers have been assessing you during the interview to establish if you are the right person for the practice, but remember that this is a two-way process. You should also be weighing up if this is the job or the practice for you. Be sure you want the job, don't fall into the trap of accepting it if offered just because you are flattered that someone wants to employ you.

Every interview is a learning opportunity even if you are not offered the job. Always analyse the interview, think about what went well and not so well, and how you would react next time. Learn from the experience.

Summary

- Prepare carefully for the interview, find out as much as possible about the practice and the job.
- Think about the questions you may be asked and the questions you will ask.
- Dress appropriately.
- Be aware of your own and the interviewer's body language.
- Be assertive and positive.
- Make an interview checklist of the things you need to remember on the day of the interview.
- Take the opportunity to show the interviewers how good you will be at the job.

What the interviewees say

Maeve – Veterinary Surgeon   *Rowena – Receptionist*
Vanessa – Nurse/Receptionist   *Lisa – Nurse*

Q: How did you prepare for the interview?

Maeve – Well, I had the practice profile so I had lots of information to go on. I thought of the likely questions I might be asked and I tried to be mentally prepared, very positive and so on.

Vanessa – I got my husband to ask me the sort of questions I thought I would be asked at the interview.

Rowena – I read the job description very carefully.

Lisa – I thought about what I wanted to say and the questions I might be asked. I looked for things that were interesting about myself that I could tell the interviewers.

Q: How did you dress for the interview?

Maeve – I thought I should be smart so I wore trousers and a smart jacket – smart casual, I suppose.

Rowena – A smart suit.

Lisa – Smartly, I knew I would be wearing a smart uniform so I tried to mirror that in my dress.

Vanessa – A suit and not too much make-up.

Q: How did you decide what questions you wanted to ask?

Maeve – By reading the practice profile; and I also had specific housekeeping questions I wanted to ask.

Vanessa – Actually most were answered in the job description.

Lisa – I needed to know more about the actual hours I would be working, but the rest of the questions were answered during the interview.

Q: How did you find out more about the practice?

Maeve – I simply went by the practice profile.

Vanessa – I knew the practice because I am a client.

Lisa – I knew the practice, but if I hadn't I would have gone along to see it.

Q: How did you cope with nerves?

Maeve – I was nervous to start with, but once the interview started I was fine, it was very relaxed and friendly.

Vanessa – I have got less nervous as I have become older, I just try to be myself and not pretend I am someone I am not.

Lisa – I was very nervous, I had not had a proper interview before; all my other interviews were very informal. I wasn't at all sure what to expect. I had been given interview practice at school but that did not really help. However, the nurse who showed me round before the interview really put me at my ease and some of my butterflies went away.

Q: What impression of the practice did you leave with?

Lisa – Very friendly.

Rowena – A nice place to work and take your pet.

Vanessa – I would recommend it to my friends. They spent time with us, they came over as nice friendly people.

10

The New Employee's First Day

Where do I go? Who do I see? What do I do? These are just some of the questions the new employee on their first day at work will be asking. It is the employer's/manager's job to answer these quickly and effectively, so that the first day does not turn into a nightmare.

Carefully planned and organised induction training for all new employees is essential if new employees are going to settle into the practice smoothly. Having spent a large amount of time and effort recruiting the right person for the job it is important to ensure that the new employee is properly inducted into their role in the practice.

A good induction process increases the new employee's progress towards satisfactory work performance, reduces the possibility of misunderstandings and conflict and the disillusion some employees experience with a new job.

Induction is all about the steps and training an employer can take to ensure that new recruits settle into their jobs quickly, happily and confidently.

The induction of employees in fact starts with the recruitment and selection process. The work expectations new employees have about their jobs, and the ideas and impressions they form are largely gained during their recruitment process. This pre-employment induction will have succeeded if the new employee can look forward to their first day with confidence and be able to say at the end of the day that it was very much as they had expected.

Pre-employment information and induction

Before starting work the new employee should receive as much relevant information about the practice and their job as possible so that they are as well prepared as they can be for their first day at work. The recruitment process will have provided them with a job description, information about the practice from the brochure and website, and they will have formed a general impression of the practice while being interviewed. The letter of appointment should have given them a starting date, time and location, but once they accept the post, it is important to provide help and information to ease them into their new role

Accommodation

If the practice provides housing for the new employee all the necessary details should be sorted out before the first day. Normally the employee would be moving into the accommodation a day or two before they start work, so that they can settle into the locality. A bunch of flowers and a bowl of fruit left in the flat or house are a welcoming gesture.

If, as is common for nurses, night duty involves staying in the practice flat, all the details of how the rota operates and what the accommodation comprises, rules and regulations, food, cooking and sleeping arrangements should be explained.

If no accommodation is provided, it may be helpful to a new employee who is moving from another area to send them details of estate agents and perhaps the property pages of the local paper to give them a start with house hunting. Some local information about the area would also be useful.

Car

Fewer practices now provide cars with the job, but if they do the new recruit needs to have details of the car, when it can be picked up and the regulations attached to its use.

Car parking facilities for employees should be explained to new employees, so that on their first day they do not make the mistake of parking in the senior partner's parking space and face the embarrassment of being asked to move their car by an irate veterinary surgeon!

Uniform and equipment

All uniform requirements, badges and equipment need to be organised before the first day so that the new recruit really feels part of the practice from day one and doesn't have to wait a week before their uniform arrives just to discover that the supplier has sent the wrong size.

Rota
It is only fair to give the new employee a copy of the practice rota as soon as possible so that they are able to plan their life. This is especially important for veterinary surgeons who may not take up the post for one or two months.

Contract of employment
The contract or conditions of employment is an important document, both legally and also because it will play an important part in the applicant's decision whether or not to accept the job. This is why it is advisable to send the contract with the job offer letter. If the potential recruit is not happy with the conditions they have the opportunity to discuss them with the employer before the job has been accepted, and if problems cannot be resolved they can refuse the job. If you wait to give the contract until after the new employee has started work and they then do not like the conditions life could become difficult.

Legislation allows conditions and contracts of employment to be issued to new employees any time within the first two months of employment. However, for the reasons above it is very much better to issue the contract with the job offer, then all is signed and sealed before the new employee starts work.

Veterinary organisations such as BSAVA, BVA and SPVS have all produced examples of employment contracts, which can be used as reference points when drawing up the practice contract. It is always advisable however to seek some legal advice when drawing up a contract for the first time just to ensure that you have included everything that is necessary and not left any loopholes.

A standard contract of employment will contain the following information:
◆ name of employer
◆ name of employee
◆ date and commencement of employment
◆ job title and/or brief job description
◆ the place or places of work

◆ scale or rate of pay and any benefits
◆ intervals when remuneration is paid
◆ terms and conditions relating to hours of work
◆ terms and conditions relating to holidays and holiday pay
◆ terms and conditions relating to sickness absence and sick pay
◆ terms and conditions relating to pensions
◆ notice periods
◆ disciplinary and grievance procedures.

The employer and the employee should sign two copies of the contract and each should keep a copy.

First day structure

Make sure the new employee knows what to expect on their first day. They need to know the following.

⇨ Which day and what time to arrive for work.
⇨ Where to report: reception, practice manager's office etc, and which surgery if there a number of branches.
⇨ Who to report to.
⇨ What is going to happen. Hopefully, details of the induction programme, described later, and not a quick hello from the senior partner and then straight into the consulting room or operating theatre.

First day induction

Who carries out the first day induction depends on the post the employee is moving into. Generally speaking, this would be the responsibility of a practice manager or personnel officer. However it involves more than just these members of staff as we shall see.

The checklist

It is very useful to have a first day checklist as shown in figure 13. The checklist acts as a handy reference to all the documentation and information that needs to be given to the new employee on their first day. Once information has been given it can be ticked off the checklist. It is helpful for both employee and employer to have copies of the checklists and to sign when information has been given or received. This avoids the, 'I was never given/told that' scenario. This handing over of documentation and provision of information, such as fire and first aid regulations is best dealt with at the start of the day so that the

Figure 13   Induction checklist

Item	Employee signature	Employer signature	Date
P45			
Personal details – next of kin, telephone numbers			
Bank details			
Payment details			
Doctor's details			
Contract if not already given			
Rota if not already given			
Keys			
Induction training programme			
Practice manual			
Discipline/ grievance procedures			
Confidentiality			
Staff training schedules and procedures			
Health and safety briefing			
First aid and fire procedures			
Domestic information – working issues, personal use of phone, e-mail			
Other information etc			

induction process can then progress to more interesting aspects of the employee's role in the practice.

First day induction programme

The most important aspect of the first day is that there should be no work for the new employee to do. This day is set aside for the employee to have time for thinking and absorbing information about the practice. It should be devoted to handing over necessary information and documentation, meeting staff and observing working procedures in different parts of the practice, as well as some personal time for the employee.

Having a formal induction programme for the day is a good way of achieving this. Figure 14 shows the kind of timetable which could be devised for a new nurse but this can be adapted for any new member of staff.

If possible, allocate a member of staff as mentor or buddy to each new employee. This provides your new recruit with someone to whom they can talk, and ask questions without feeling awkward or embarrassed. It also takes some of the pressure from the busy practice manager, head nurse, or head receptionist in whose department the new recruit may be about to work. For new veterinary surgeons, a partner often carries out the mentoring, but it may well be worth considering also having another named assistant to act as a buddy with whom the new person can have a less formal relationship.

General induction training

Induction training should not be confused with job training. Induction training introduces new employees to the staff, the practice and the culture of the workplace, sets out general practice standards, often deals with much of the health and safety training, and familiarises the employee with the roles of the other members of staff by work shadowing.

Job training is just what it says, it trains the employee how to do the job. A successful induction programme should integrate with the training and development plan for the individual. Induction should run alongside job training and the eventual transition between the two should be seamless.

It is very important to understand each other's roles if there is to be effective and efficient communication between staff. This is why much

Figure 14	First day induction programme for trainee nurse

Induction programme

Programme for............................. Date................

9.00 – 10.00	Meet practice manger to receive documentation and information briefing
10.00 – 10.30	Practice tour with mentor/buddy, to meet staff, etc
10.30 – 11.00	Coffee with head nurse
11.00 – 12.30	Observation in ops, hospital, kennels
12.30 – 1.00	Private time
1.00 – 2.00	Lunch with mentor/buddy
2.00 – 4.00	Observation in reception, admin., sales area, etc
4.00 – 4.30	Private time
4.30 – 5.00	Review of day with practice manager

Figure 15			Induction training checklist
Training	Date training completed	Employer signature	Employee signature
Health and safety Fire First aid Personal protective equipment COSHH etc			
Work shadowing Reception Client records Appointment booking etc			
Observing consultations			
Visiting branch surgeries			
Work shadowing Nursing Puppy parties Nurses clinics Practice nurse consultations Etc.			
Client-care training			
Assertiveness training			
Other etc			

of the induction programme – which may last from one to four weeks, depending on the role of the employee and the size of the practice – will involve work-shadowing colleagues in other disciplines.

The best way to ensure that the new employee receives their full induction is to produce an induction rota so that there is time allocated for the different induction activities. A part of most days for the first few weeks should be given over to induction. This may seem a lot of time lost in job training but in the long term it is well worth spending the time. As a result the employee is fully versed in the workings of the practice and understands work problems from their colleagues' point of view.

To be sure that induction has actually happened an induction training checklist can be drawn up as shown in figure 15, which is for a nurse. As each area of the training is completed the practice

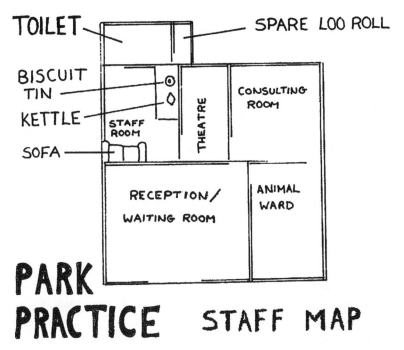

TOILET

SPARE LOO ROLL

BISCUIT
TIN

KETTLE

SOFA

STAFF
ROOM

THEATRE

CONSULTING
ROOM

RECEPTION/
WAITING ROOM

ANIMAL
WARD

PARK
PRACTICE   STAFF MAP

manager/head of department and the employee should sign the check-list.

The induction needs of particular groups of new employees

Whatever induction programme has been set up by the practice, it will need to be revisited and probably revised for certain groups of employees who will require different or more specialist induction. The main groups that the practice may have to deal with are discussed below.

School leavers and young trainees

School leavers and young trainees aged 18 years and under will require a more thorough induction training. This is because in general they lack experience in the ways of work and the requirements needed to carry out their job. Their lack of experience and youth may also expose them to greater health and safety risks, and they are likely to be less careful than an older, more experienced member of staff.

They will require more careful supervision and will most definitely benefit from having an older buddy or mentor. They will probably also need more encouragement and reassurance that they are doing the job well and fitting into the practice.

Returners to work

Don't assume that someone returning to work will be able to simply just pick up where they left off even only three or four years ago. The veterinary world is changing fast, both clinically and in its business procedures. Returners to work will need time to adjust to these changes. The practice culture may have changed and information technology will have developed in leaps and bounds. There will be new equipment and formal training may not have been the norm when the new employee was last working in a veterinary practice. Consider all these aspects when designing the induction programme for this group of people.

Part timers

Part timers have often been called the 'Cinderallas' of the employment world, never benefiting in the same way as full-time employees or being considered as important. This is changing, especially with new employment legislation relating to part-time employees but it is still important to consider the difficulties they may face. It is important to make them feel part of the practice.

It can be difficult to feel part of the practice when you only work three mornings a week, so there has to be a big effort made to address this. One of the best ways is to be sure that they are kept as well informed as the full-time employees. Explain during induction how this will be done and make them feel as valued as their full-time counterparts.

Without part-time employees veterinary practices would be struggling to cover the sort of hours they must keep open. There will be more training difficulties for part-time staff as they will not always be around for organised training sessions. How this problem is solved is up to the individual practice, but solved it must be if the employee's full potential is to be reached and they don't begin to feel a 'second class citizen' who misses out on everything.

Job sharers

Job sharers have similar work problems to part-timers. They also have to be very good communicators and organisers for the job share to be successful. They must understand how their job share works and have joint responsibility for the whole job. This needs to be emphasised during the induction process and constantly monitored during the first few months of work.

Employees with disabilities
Disabled employees may have very special needs and they should be introduced to the new job with this always in mind. Employees with hearing needs may require special telephones, partially sighted employees may need special computer screens. Less mobile employees will require more space for moving around and possibly ramps provided. Some of this is a matter of being prepared and consulting with a new employee about their requirements, so that you are prepared when they arrive.

Any employee with learning difficulties will require very special training and the jobs that they are able to do carefully assessed. The safety of disabled employees may need more attention and special induction in health and safety may be required.

Promotions and job changes
We often overlook this group of employees because they are already working for us. However, their induction needs are just as important as those of the new recruit. They may be moving to a different practice in the group, be taking on more responsibility, be working with new colleagues and have a different line of responsibility. This is really very little different from being a new employee and their induction process should be designed with this in mind.

Reviewing and revising induction
Induction is a continuing process. The practice and its working procedures will change and induction needs to be altered in line with these changes. It is also useful to get feedback from newly inducted employees to find out how well the induction process worked for them. In the same way, ask trainers how well the system works and what suggestions they have for improvements. Do not be afraid to change anything which does not work.

Monitor the induction process so that changes are made when necessary, in order to provide the best possible introduction to the practice for the new employee and adapt the process to the needs of the individual.

If you get the induction process right you will be well on the way to creating a happy and motivated workforce.

Summary

- A good induction process increases the chances of a good working relationship with new employees.
- Good induction increases commitment and motivation.
- Provide as much pre-employment information and documentation as possible for the new employee to ensure that they are confident on their first day.
- Give the contract of employment before the start of the job.
- A first day checklist helps to make sure you have provided the new employee with all the necessary first day information.
- Do not ask the new employee to work on their first day.
- Devise a first day induction programme for the new employee and make sure they see it before their first day.
- Do not confuse induction training with job training.
- Carry out general induction training over the first few weeks.
- Have an induction training checklist and record when training has been satisfactorily carried out.
- Consider and provide for the induction needs of particular groups of people.
- Revise and review your induction process on a regular basis.

What the new employees say

Maeve – Veterinary Surgeon   *Rowena – Receptionist*
Vanessa – Nurse/Receptionist   **Lisa** *– Nurse*

Q: How did you feel on your first day?

Maeve – I felt a bit lost and anxious, but much better once I started to talk to people and get going.

Lisa – Nervous, but I knew that I would be shown around and only expected to watch on the first day and that helped.

Rowena – I felt quite confident, I knew what to expect from talking to the practice and the information they sent me.

Vanessa – I was really looking forward to it.

Q: What help were you given on the first day?

Maeve – I had all the protocols and pamphlets and I received lots of help and support from the other vets and support staff. I didn't feel awkward about asking anyone if I had any difficulties.

Lisa – I was given health and safety information and we talked about the rota and the practice. I found this very helpful. I watched some operations and was shown some of the basic routines by other staff

Rowena – I had my induction checklist and ticked off things as I was told them or received them. I was also given my training folder and health and safety instruction.

Vanessa – Lots! Everyone was very friendly I was shown around and I felt very comfortable. There was nothing else that I think they could have done.

Q: How did you feel at the end of the first day?

Maeve – Exhausted. I went to bed early. But in fact it was not as bad as I had expected, although I obviously had lots to learn. Having the induction was very helpful but I have to say that learning by 'doing it yourself' cannot be beaten.

Lisa – I felt very good and a lot more confident.

Rowena – I felt fine and was looking forward to the next day.

Vanessa – I felt fine, I knew I had made the right decision and I was going to enjoy the job.

11

Probationary Periods and Appraisals

Probationary periods

For most staff there is a six-month probationary period when they are first employed by a practice. This is in effect an assessment time both for the employer and employee. It is the time for the employer to decide if this is the right person for the job, will they fit in, can they do the job, do they get on well with the clients? And it is for the employee to make up their minds whether this is the right job for them. Do they like it, can they do it, do they get on with the rest of the staff, is it what they thought it would be at the interview?

It is very important for the employer to make the best use of this probationary period and really find out if they have recruited success-fully. If the answer is yes then all is well, but if the answer is no, action needs to be taken and quickly. Once an employee has been employed by the practice for more than twelve months, dismissal procedures become very difficult and complicated. It is therefore vital that if the wrong person has been chosen, and they cannot do the job to the required standards, or there are other reasons why the practice does not want to continue to employ them, they are removed within the twelve-month period.

There are countless veterinary practices in the country whose man-agers or principals have said about a new employee 'They will improve with time' or 'Let's wait and see for a little bit longer' or 'They are a really nice person, they are trying their best we should give them a chance'. These are kind and charitable words, but the chances are that these employees will not improve. They may be lovely people, but if they can't do the job they are not a lot of use to the practice. This may

seem harsh but at the end of the day
the responsibility of the manager is
to run the practice as efficiently and
effectively as possible and this does
not mean carrying under-achieving
or problem staff. The words 'If
only we had told them to leave
before the twelve months were up'
must have been on many a manager's lips!

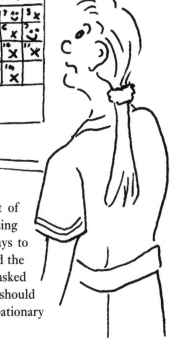

It is true that some employees take longer to settle down
than others and that their true
potential takes longer to develop. This must of
course be taken into consideration when assessing
how well they are doing. One of the best ways to
assess the success of the new recruit and avoid the
mistake of keeping them when they should be asked
to leave, or asking them to leave when they should
have been kept, is to have in place a probationary
appraisal system.

Probationary appraisals

Probationary appraisals are in fact part of any induction process.
Ideally they should be carried out at one, three and six months intervals, at which time a decision should be made about the employee's
future.

Probationary appraisals have a number of advantages to both
employer and employee.

Advantages to the employer

⇨ They provide a formal assessment of the work and aptitudes of
   new employee.
⇨ They provide a forum for discussion of any problems or
   difficulties, real or perceived, by both employer and employee.
⇨ They identify problems quickly.
⇨ They provide a good introduction to the formal annual appraisal
   system.
⇨ They can forestall any serious discipline or grievance issues by
   sorting out difficulties before they reach serious proportions.

⇨ They provide a record of the employee's work and achievements and allow for better planning of training needs.

⇨ If done well, they help to bond the employee to the practice and increase work productivity and motivation.

Advantages to the employee

⇨ They provide reassurance that the employee is doing the job well or that they will receive help to improve their standards.

⇨ They show that the employer cares about how the employee is faring.

⇨ They identify problems quickly and enable them to be resolved before they get out of proportion in the employee's mind.

⇨ They allow for a fixed discussion time about the employee's job.

⇨ They can be used to sort out personal problems or difficulties at work.

⇨ They are an opportunity to discuss anything about the employee's role in the practice, job, staff relations, training, etc.

⇨ They are confidential.

Who should carry out these appraisals?

Ideally the employee's line manager should carry out their probationary appraisals. It should be someone with whom the employee feels comfortable but who has a working knowledge of how they are doing their job. It may be that the practice manager and the employee's immediate supervisor act as appraisers, but it is likely that it is the supervisor who will have the most input into the appraisal in terms of assessment of working standards and interpersonal skills.

What does the appraisal look at?

The probationary appraisal should look at least some of the following areas.

The work output and productivity of the employee

How well do they work? Are they producing the results you require? Do they work hard enough?

The quality of the work

Is it of the standard required?

The employee's attitude

What sort of attitude do they have to work and to colleagues? Is it appropriate?

The employee's relationship with other staff

How well does the employee get on with the rest of the staff?

Client–care skills

How well does the employee relate to clients and provide good client care?

The employee's competence

Is the employee competent at their job?

Attendance and punctuality record

How punctual is the employee? What is their attendance record? Are there any problems?

It is helpful to design an appraisal form which asks these questions, for the appraiser to complete before the day of the appraisal. Many practices adopt a system whereby a copy of this completed form will be given to the employee to be appraised so that they can read and consider the comments before the interview.

The employee should also be provided with a self-appraisal form to complete. A copy of this form can be given to the appraisers a few days before the interview. This will enable them to read and consider the areas the employee has highlighted.

The self-appraisal form should be asking the employee questions like these.

⇨ How well does the employee think they are carrying out their role?

⇨ Does the employee fully understand what their job entails?

⇨ Which areas of the job does the employee think they carry out best?

⇨ Which areas, if any, do they have difficulty with?

⇨ Which areas do they most enjoy?

⇨ Is there anything which is making it difficult for them to carry out their job?

⇨ Does the employee have any skills which they think could be better used in the practice?

⇨ Is there any particular training that the employee feels they would benefit from?

⇨ How well does the employee think they get on with other members of staff? Are there any difficulties?

⇨ How well does the employee feel they get on with clients? Are there any difficulties?

⇨ Are there any other areas of working in the practice, or the job that the employee would like to discuss?

It is important that the appraisal process is fully explained to the new employee. It is helpful to mention the appraisal system at the interview so that the employee is already aware that the practice adopts the probationary appraisal procedure. The employee should understand what the appraisals are for, what is involved, the part they play and how formal or informal they will be. The more informal these probationary appraisals are the better. They should not be made into the 'Spanish Inquisition'; the purpose of the appraisal is to help and encourage, not to terrify.

Carrying out the appraisal

There is no set procedure for carrying out appraisals but a good guide would be to follow the steps below.

1 Explain the system. Be sure that the employee understands the reason for the appraisal, how the forms are used and what happens as a result of the appraisal.

2 Distribute the self-appraisal form to the employee at least a week before the appraisal and explain how you expect it to be completed.

3 Distribute the appraisal form to the appraisers at least a week before the appraisal.

4 Allow time for forms to be exchanged and considered.

5 Hold the appraisal interview.

6 Agree the actions to be taken as a result of the interview.

7 Write a letter to the employee setting out the main points of the interview and the actions which will be taken.

8 Review the actions identified at the next appraisal.

The appraisal interview is like any other interview in terms of venue, time and privacy. Choose a quiet room where you will not be disturbed, keep the atmosphere as relaxed as possible, and allow at least an hour for the interview.

Start the interview by thanking the employee for coming and completing the self-appraisal form, then ask them if they would like to provide a resumé of what they have said in the form. Ask them to elaborate further on any points of difficulty.

Before agreeing what actions need to be taken to resolve any problems, the appraiser should sum up the points made on the appraisal form and give the employee a chance to discuss any area where they perhaps may not agree or wish to discuss further.

At the end of these discussions everyone should agree on the actions that need to be taken by both the employer and employee. The main points of the interview and the agreed actions should be put in writing and a copy given to the employee.

At the next appraisal these action points should be discussed. The questions that need to be asked are: have the actions been carried out, did they work, what effect has there been, should they be continued?

Probationary appraisals can of course simply take the form of a general chat with the employee or perhaps the completion of a very simple form or just the taking of notes. The style in which appraisals are carried out is very much up to the individual practice. The important thing is that they happen and are acted upon so that any difficulties are addressed in the first few months of the new member of staff's employment.

Naturally it is hoped that at the six-month appraisal the employer will be able to congratulate the employee on how they are progressing and confirm that the probationary period is at an end. Sadly this is not always going to be the case. The sort of problems which arise with new employees and how to deal with them are discussed in the following chapter 12

Summary

- Probationary periods should be used to assess the skills and suitability of new employees.
- Probationary appraisals are a very good way to assess the suitability of new staff.
- The use of appraisal forms for the employee's self appraisal and employer's appraisal greatly help the appraisal process.
- Treat the appraisal interview like any other interview allowing at least an hour for its completion.
- Decide on the actions to be taken as a result of the interview.
- Always put the results of the interview in writing and give a copy to the employee.
- If this is not the right person for the practice be decisive and end their employment before they have been with the practice for twelve months.

What the interviewees say

Maeve – Veterinary Surgeon   *Rowena – Receptionist*
Vanessa – Nurse/Receptionist   *Lisa – Nurse*

Q: Do you think probationary appraisals are helpful?

Maeve – Yes, it really helps to talk on a more formal basis, but I feel that I can do this with my employer informally at any time.

Rowena – Yes, it's important to know how you are doing and that you are working in the right way. They help to give you more confidence in yourself.

Lisa – They are very helpful. My job changed quite soon after I came to the practice because at the appraisal we discussed how else some of my skills could be used. I'm now doing much more interesting work that I was originally employed to do. I don't think this would have happened so quickly if there had not been appraisals where I could discuss the job.

Vanessa – Yes, they are very good. They allowed me to talk about problems I had and to work out how to solve them as soon as possible. It was also good to be told officially how I was doing.

What the interviewers say

Q: What are the advantages to the employer of probationary appraisals?

Mary – It's good for bonding the employee to the practice. It shows them we care about them and how they are doing. But of course it's good for the employer because we can sort out problems at the very start – before they get too serious – and we can change or increase any areas of training if the employee has difficulties. It allows us to say 'Well done, you're doing fine' or perhaps, 'We need some improvement here'. Either way, the employee knows where they stand and that we are taking time to see how they are doing and not just leaving them to 'get on with it'.

Denise – It helps to know how people see their job, how they feel about it and what help they need. I think it is also good for them to know that you are behind them and will help them where you can, I think it makes them more committed.

12

What can go wrong

The best laid plans can still go wrong. However well you interview and select employees there will always be times when you simply choose the wrong person. The important thing is not to regard this as a failure, but to simply put it down to experience, and learn from that experience. If you have employed the wrong person, act quickly to remedy the situation.

So, what can go wrong? There may be discipline problems, it may be that the person simply is not up to the job and training is not going to help, or it may simply be that they do not fit in with the practice and its staff.

Discipline

Every veterinary practice should have a written copy of their disciplinary procedure. This should be available to, and preferably given to, all members of staff when they commence employment. The procedure should set out what constitutes misconduct and the procedures the practice goes through if a member of staff is considered to have breached these rules. The objective of any disciplinary rules and procedures are to maintain the standards of the veterinary practice and the main areas where discipline must be enforced are

◆ attendance
◆ job capabilities
◆ safety
◆ behaviour
◆ honesty.

Before we go any further however, a word of warning: ALWAYS

seek legal advice before carrying out any procedure which may ultimately end in possible staff dismissal or dispute. Employment law is a minefield for the manager and the law is constantly changing. There are numerous free legal advice lines available to the veterinary profession, BVA Legal Line and VPMA Legal Advice Line, to name but two. Take the time to check with these advisors before you plunge into any form of disciplinary or other potentially legally hazardous employment exercise. Legal help lines are a good starting point for advice, much better take time to ask for advice at the beginning of an employment problem, than be faced with huge sums to pay in compensation and legal fees at the end of a court case.

Discipline, or the lack of it, is normally divided in two categories:
◆ misconduct
◆ gross misconduct.
These two terms should be very clearly defined in the practice disciplinary procedure, so that staff are completely aware of what is and is not acceptable behaviour in the practice.

Misconduct
Generally speaking misconduct arises when the employee has a persistent or serious problem in one of the following areas:
◆ attendance
◆ work standards
◆ health and safety
◆ confidentiality
◆ carrying out instructions
◆ behaviour
◆ non co-operation
◆ off-duty conduct
  which could bring
  the practice into
  disrepute.

Gross misconduct

Gross misconduct would be considered to any of the following:

◆ theft
◆ falsification of records
◆ fraud
◆ assault
◆ malicious damage
◆ abuse on the premises of drugs/alcohol
◆ serious negligence.

If your new member of staff is still within their twelve-month employment period, you are within your rights to give them notice if you find their behaviour unacceptable. The other option is to carry out a disciplinary hearing, in the hope that this will solve the problem and the member of staff will be retained. The choice of option is the decision of the practice. However do bear in mind that time is not on your side. A disciplinary hearing is not a quick process, especially if the employee appeals against your decision. Remember that you will also have to give a period of notice which could be one month, thus bringing the actual time with the practice down to eleven months. Once they have been with you for twelve months dismissal is quite another ball game. Also, care is needed as to whether the disciplinary procedure is contractual or not. If it is deemed to be, then it must be followed to the letter.

If a disciplinary hearing is chosen the matter must be investigated fully and the practice disciplinary procedure must be strictly followed. The member of staff should be interviewed before the hearing, as should any other members of staff concerned. The evidence should be assessed and if appropriate a disciplinary meeting held and all conclusions confirmed in writing to the employee. The checklist shows the basic procedures to follow during a disciplinary procedure. Always remember that what you initially think may be a disciplinary action might turn out to be only the need for advice, help or counselling. This is why a thorough investigation into the problem is so important.

Technical abilities

Assessing a new employee's technical/clinical abilities and their ability to work with, and relate to, clients can sometimes be difficult. It is relatively easy to asses how well a good employee is doing and just as easy to assess the poor member of staff. It is the ones in the 'middle' that are

---

Disciplinary procedure   Checklist

Gather facts
- ❑   promptly
- ❑   take statements

Be clear about the complaint
- ❑   do you need to take action?

Decide action
- ❑   advice?
- ❑   counselling?
- ❑   disciplinary action?

---

difficult and the questions are always – 'Will they improve?' or 'If we give them more time will they get better?' and 'Are we not training them well enough?'

The probationary appraisals will help the manager answer some of these questions, but eventually the time will come to make the go or stay decision. Ask yourself the following questions.

How much extra training do they need?

Can we provide it?

Will this be economic?

Realistically, will it work?

Do you really think that they will eventually be able to do the job?

Do we want to go to this trouble?

What has been the feedback from the employee?

What enthusiasm do they have to improve?

Will they be better off in a different job?

No one likes to dismiss staff. It is usually an embarrassing and difficult exercise, but sometimes it is the only solution. Never keep an unsuitable new member of staff because you feel sorry for them or cannot face the prospect of dismissing them. In many cases you may be doing them a favour, as they will move to work in jobs which are more suitable for them and which they enjoy better. (Even vets can have successful second careers.)

Fitting in to the practice

This is perhaps the most difficult reason to give to a new employee for a dismissal but it is a very important one as far as the practice is concerned. It illustrates how important it is to make sure that interviewees meet as many members of staff as possible before they are offered the job. How good a worker the new employee is, or how good they are technically, does not matter if they cannot get on with the rest of the staff. Disharmony among staff is one of the greatest demotivators. One bad apple can turn many of the others rotten, remove the apple before this can happen.

It is not necessarily the fault of the new employee that the others do not get on with them and, if indeed this is the case, the manager has no choice but to consider the good of the practice first. They will have to tell the new employee that they do not think they 'gell' with the rest of the practice or that they are not fitting in as a team member. However this is expressed, it should be done with care and sensitivity.

Discrimination

The manager must be very careful that the reasons for dismissal are not discriminatory and cannot be interpreted as such by the employee or their solicitor. Discrimination was discussed in earlier chapters and all the grounds for discrimination mentioned there apply for dismissal. Remember also that even if you wish to dismiss an employee who has been with you for less than twelve months on totally appropriate grounds, where ill health or pregnancy are involved they may prejudice the case for dismissal. So it is wise, even if you think you are totally within your rights as an employer to dismiss, to seek legal advice BEFORE you take any action leading to a dismissal.

Parting company

In an ideal world you wish to part company with your employee on good terms. This is of course not always possible. Remember that the dismissal procedure, just like the recruitment procedure, has an important PR dimension. Any employee who leaves on bad terms will not be a good advocate for the practice.

Sometimes leaving is a mutual decision and both employee and employer understand that this was the wrong person for the job. Sometimes it is the employee who wants to leave and the employer who wants them to stay.

If possible conduct an exit interview with the employee, particularly if you both agree that the appointment was a mistake. The exit interview will give you some insight into what went wrong and how you can improve interviewing techniques, as well as perhaps induction procedures. It may give you even more useful information about the practice, both good and bad. Exit interviews with antagonistic staff are unlikely to be very productive even supposing it is possible to carry one out.

Starting again

So you are back to square one! Well no, not really, because you will hopefully have learnt from the experience. Perhaps the job needs some modification, perhaps the person specification needs changing, or maybe you should use different interview procedures. Analyse what went wrong and learn from any mistakes. Do not be disheartened by any perceived failure, remember that this happens to everyone. The secret is to go into the next selection and interview process with a clean slate and a positive view that this time you really will get the best person for the job.

Summary

- No one gets interviewing right all of the time, we all make mistakes.
- Assess technical skills and abilities carefully during the probationary period.
- Assess how well the new employee fits in with the rest of the staff.
- Give all new employees a copy of the practice disciplinary procedures.
- If you decide to discipline the new member of staff follow disciplinary procedures very carefully.
- ALWAYS seek legal advice on any major employment matter.
- Act quickly if you intend to end an employee's contract within the twelve month period.
- Conduct exit interviews where appropriate.
- View having to repeat the interviewing process as an opportunity to find the best person for the job not as a failure.

The Last Word from Interviewers

Always send out the job description to the candidates – it saves so much time on the interview day.

Writing a personal profile for the job really helps to clarify in your mind who you are looking for.

It's worth spending time designing a professional looking advert.

I always read the CVs very carefully it's amazing what you learn form what is not said in them.

Always give yourself plenty of time for the interview, it's awful to feel rushed.

Preparing a comprehensive list of questions to ask the candidate has made a great deal of difference to my confidence in interviewing candidates.

Beware of candidates who criticise their last employer, what will they soon be saying about you?

Having a candidate assessment form was very useful for comparing candidates who were similar in their abilities.

I have to try very, very hard not to be influenced by first impressions because I have learnt that occasionally my first impression has in fact been wrong.

I always listen to staff opinion on candidates and they are usually right.

It's very important to remember that however hard you try, you will occasionally choose the wrong person for the job.

Sometimes your gut feeling really does pay off and, against all the odds, this is what makes you choose the right candidate.

The Last Word from Interviewees

Find out as much as you can about the practice and the job before the interview, it really helped me to feel more confident.

I think it is important to dress smartly for the job it shows you care about getting it

I tried to think of all the questions I might be asked and how I would answer and I guessed right in quite a few cases.

I think I benefited a great deal from my induction course I understood so much more about the practice at the end of it.

I was really nervous but I kept on thinking that the interviewers would understand this and make allowances.

It's important to show the interviewers that you really want the job and to be enthusiastic.

The first interview you have is always the worst.

Index

Useful Addresses

British Psychological Society
St Andrew's House
48 Princess Road East
Leicester LE 1 7DR
Tel 0116 2549568
Website www.bps.org.uk

British Small Animal Veterinary Association
Woodrow House
1 Telford Way
Waterwells Business Park
Quedgeley
Gloucestershire GL 2 4BA
Tel: 01452 726700
website: www.bsava.co
email: adminoff@bsava.com

British Veterinary Association
7 Mansfield Street
London W1M 0AT
Tel: 0207 636 6541
website: www.bva.co.uk

British Veterinary Nursing Association
Level 15 Terminus House
Terminus Street
Harlow, Essex CM 20 1XA
Tel: 01279 450567
email: bvna@compuserve.com

Criminal Records Bureau
Customer Services
CRB
PO Box 110
Tel 0870 90 90 811
Website http://www.crb.gov.uk

Federation of Small Businesses
Sir Frank Whittle Way
Blackpool Business Park
Blackpool
Lancashire FY 4 2FE
Tel 01253 336000
Fax 01253 348046
Member's email legal@fsb.org.uk
Non-member's membership@fsb.org.uk
Website http://www.fsb.org.uk

HSE Books
PO Box 1999
Sudbury
Suffolk CO 10 6FS
Tel: 01787 881165

Health and Safety Executive
Information Centre
Broad Lane
Sheffield S 3 7HQ
Tel: 0541 545500
www.open.gov.uk./hse/hsehome.htm

Institute of Personnel and Development
IPD House
35 Camp Road
Wimbledon
London SW 19 4UX
Tel 020 8971 9000
Website www.ipd.co.uk

Royal College of Veterinary Surgeons
Belgravia House
62–64 Horseferry Road
London SW 1P 2AF
Tel: 0207 222 2001
email: admin@rcvs.org.uk
website: www.rcvs.org.uk/rcvs/

Veterinary Practice Management
  Association
76 St John's Road
Kettering
Northants NN 15 5AZ
Tel 07000 782324
Fax 01933 399723
E-mail secretariat@vpma.co.uk
Website www.vpma.co.uk

Also by Maggie Shilcock
The Veterinary Support Team

What a pity this book was not written before I became a practice manager! ... an easy-to-read style... a must for practice libraries and for those considering joining a veterinary practice.

Penny Bredemear *VN Times*

..this book is a starting point for providing the veterinary support team with the training tools that they need. ...for new entrants into and the progressing members of the veterinary support team.

Christine Ann Merle DVM MB *Editorial@penguin.doody.com*

A comprehensive and practical discussion of the role of veterinary support staff and their importance to the practice—invaluable for support staff, practice managers and vets. The author, an experienced practice administrator, gives concise advice in a clear text, with plenty of diagrams and drawings.

Key topics include: how support staff create and influence the practice image, how to create co-operative support staff teams. The discussion is balanced by comments from working support staff about their jobs.

CONTENTS

Who are they and what do they do? – The practice image – Client care skills – Assertiveness and dealing with difficult clients – Support staff and money – Support staff and the office – How support staff contribute to sales and marketing – Support staff and the law – Support staff and the clinical role – Teamwork – Understanding other roles – Surviving in veterinary practice – The future

Price	£14.95 (paperback)	**Publication**	2001
Format	216 x 138 mm	**Extent**	144 pp
ISBN	1-903152-06-2	Distributed in N. America by Iowa State Press	

The Pocket Practice Guides

Clients, Pets and Vets   Carl Gorman MRCVS

This is the book that every new graduate trembling on the morning of their first day in companion animal practice needs to have read - ideally twice. Mike Dale MRCVS *The Veterinary Record*

I very much enjoyed reading this book. ...an invaluable guide for dealing with clients for anyone in veterinary practice at the 'sharp end' of client communication and handling. This is sensible, basic and very helpful advice on dealing with clients.

Veterinary Management for Today

Carl Gorman's book provides advice and food for thought in the pitfall-strewn field of client management. The core message of the book is the importance of communication. Communication with colleagues, lay staff and, most vitally, with clients. Keeping clients informed is the best way of keeping clients happy.

By demonstrating some areas where communications can break down, and the reasons why, *Clients, Pets and Vets* enables you to look after clients and so fully enjoy your time in practice and maximise your potential.

CONTENTS

Why do we need clients? – Making clients feel at home – Making your message understood – Clients have pets as well – The art of persuasion – How to look good – How to break bad news – Awkward situations – Euthanasia – How to be a helpful client

Price	£14.95 (paperback)	Publication	2000
Format	216 x 138 mm	Extent	176 pp
ISBN	1-903152-04-6	Distributed in N. America by Iowa State Press	

Second edition

Finance, Employment and Wealth for Vets
Keith Dickinson

..an excellent pocket guide to the fundamentals of the commercial world of veterinary practice. I strongly recommend this book for the practice bookshelf.   Paul Manning *Veterinary Times*

I wish I had this source of information available to me at graduation. It would have made life a lot easier. It is logically laid out and quite accessible for financial information.   A recently-qualified MRCVS

Within a year of first publication, Keith Dickinson, a leading adviser to vets on finance, has already fully updated his useful practical guide for newly-qualified vets and everyone in the profession who is concerned about financial and employment issues.

His discussion of pensions, mortgages, savings and insurance focuses on the key issues for you as a vet or manager: sorting out your priorities whatever the dizzying range of products available.

CONTENTS

Joining the veterinary profession – A salary guide – The interview – Employment packages & taxation – Entitlements of employment – Employee benefits – Pensions – Mortgages – Personal savings – Personal financial protection – Insurance – Interviews with four vets – What next?

Price	£14.95 (paperback)	**Second edition**	2001
Format	216 x 138 mm	**Extent**	144 pp
ISBN	1-903152-08-9		

Premises for Vets
Designing the Veterinary Habitat

Jim Wishart DipM MCIM AMCIPD FInstSMM

A re you making the best use of your premises and the space available? If you want to expand, what are your options? Jim Wishart, an established planner of veterinary premises, gives you the tools to decide.

★ The extension vs. new building decision
★ Planning effective and logical work spaces and workflows
★ Finishes, furniture and flooring for optimal environments
★ Balancing clinical and health & safety requirements with cost and maintainability
★ Selecting sites and taking on the property market
★ Working with builders, architects and developers.

CONTENTS
What Do We Want to Achieve? – Thinking and Planning – Location and Site Finding – Types of Buildings and Finishes – The Design and Building Stages – **Small Animal Premises** – Front of House – In-House Services – In-Patient Treatment – **Farm Animal and Equine Facilities** – Special Requirements of Farm and Equine Work – **Turning the Key** – Promotion and Opening

£14.95 (paperback)	2002	
216 x 138 mm	176 pp	1-903152-09-7